teach yourself®

**baby massage
and yoga**

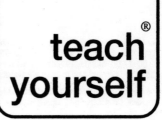

**baby massage
and yoga**
anita epple and
pauline carpenter

For over 60 years, more than
50 million people have learnt over
750 subjects the **teach yourself**
way, with impressive results.

be where you want to be
with **teach yourself**

For UK order enquiries: please contact Bookpoint Ltd, 130 Milton Park, Abingdon, Oxon, OX14 4SB. Telephone: +44 (0) 1235 827720. Fax: +44 (0) 1235 400454. Lines are open 09.00–17.00, Monday to Saturday, with a 24-hour message answering service. Details about our titles and how to order are available at www.teachyourself.co.uk.

For USA order enquiries: please contact McGraw-Hill Customer Services, PO Box 545, Blacklick, OH 43004-0545, USA. Telephone: 1-800-722-4726. Fax: 1-614-755-5645.

For Canada order enquiries: please contact McGraw-Hill Ryerson Ltd, 300 Water St, Whitby, Ontario L1N 9B6, Canada. Telephone: 905 430 5000. Fax: 905 430 5020.

Long renowned as the authoritative source for self-guided learning – with more than 50 million copies sold worldwide – the **teach yourself** series includes over 500 titles in the fields of languages, crafts, hobbies, business, computing and education.

British Library Cataloguing in Publication Data: a catalogue record for this title is available from the British Library.

Library of Congress Catalog Card Number: on file.

First published in UK 2007 by Hodder Education, 338 Euston Road, London, NW1 3BH.

First published in US 2007 by The McGraw-Hill Companies, Inc.

This edition published 2007.

The **teach yourself** name is a registered trade mark of Hodder Headline.

Copyright © 2007 Anita Epple and Pauline Carpenter

Typeset by Transet Limited, Coventry, England.
Printed in Great Britain for Hodder Education, a division of Hodder Headline, an Hachette Livre UK Company, 338 Euston Road, London, NW1 3BH, by Cox & Wyman Ltd, Reading, Berkshire.

The publisher has used its best endeavours to ensure that the URLs for external websites referred to in this book are correct and active at the time of going to press. However, the publisher and the author have no responsibility for the websites and can make no guarantee that a site will remain live or that the content will remain relevant, decent or appropriate.

Hodder Headline's policy is to use papers that are natural, renewable and recyclable products and made from wood grown in sustainable forests. The logging and manufacturing processes are expected to conform to the environmental regulations of the country of origin.

Impression number   10 9 8 7 6 5 4 3 2 1
Year   2010 2009 2008 2007

contents

dedication

To our children Kristi, Tim, Lucy, Anna, Manon and Amélie
for whom loving touch is a part of their every day lives.

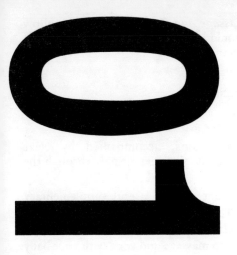

introduction

In this chapter you will learn:
- an overview of baby massage and yoga
- the history and origins of baby massage and yoga.

Teach Yourself Baby Massage and Yoga is an easy-to-follow guide for parents who would like to practise the wonderful art of massage and yoga with their babies.

The book contains:

- a full body massage routine
- a short yoga routine
- a story-time massage for the growing child.

Simple step-by-step instructions, accompanied by clear illustrations and pictures, guide you reassuringly through the massage and yoga routines.

In addition, there is a great deal of useful supplementary information to ensure that this special pleasure can be carried out safely in the comfort of your home, including:

- when is the best time to do massage and yoga with your baby
- when is not a good time
- the best oils to use
- the importance of being comfortable during the routines.

The routines are divided into bite-sized sections to aid your effective learning and build confidence, whilst giving your baby a gentle introduction to massage and yoga.

Baby massage and yoga are truly remarkable skills to learn, not only because there are a host of physical benefits but also because they help to build and strengthen a life-long relationship for you and your baby.

Before beginning the massage and yoga routines, please refer to the 'When is not a good time to do massage and yoga with your baby' (Chapter 3). If you have any questions about introducing any part of the massage strokes or yoga exercise, please seek advice from your GP or paediatrician.

Neither the authors nor the publisher can be held responsible for any injury or any other effects of the massage or yoga routines on a baby.

An explanation of baby massage and baby yoga

A general overview

Touch is one of the first senses to develop. When a baby is in the womb they experience a constant massage from their mother's gentle movements. Once born, babies need to be touched to thrive, and parents can use the powers of positive touch, such as massage and yoga, to satisfy this need and help them communicate and bond with their child.

Parents, particularly new mothers who are returning to work after the birth of their baby, often like to find activities that give them quality time with their children. Baby massage and yoga are simple and free and can be done almost anywhere; which also fits in well with parents who juggle a host of responsibilities and have hectic lifestyles.

Above all, baby massage and yoga enable parents and babies to relax and have fun together!

History and origins – baby massage

Baby massage has been a common practice in many cultures for hundreds of years. The use of massage for babies has its roots in Ayurvedic medicine in India, dating back as far as 1800 BC. To this day, families from many cultures, such as Nepal, Tibet, Malaysia and India, recognize the value of massage to promote health and a sense of well-being for the mother and child – before and after birth. Even today in some regions of India, babies are still massaged for 10–20 minutes, morning and evening until they are six months old.

Baby massage came to western society in the 1970s and has become increasingly popular since the turn of the 21st century and is now taught to parents by many health professionals and complementary therapists in the UK and USA who recognize the wonderful benefits.

History and origins – baby yoga

The origins of yoga are found in ancient history and it has been commonly practiced throughout the world for centuries. Yoga came from South West Asia more than 3,000 years ago and then migrated south through the Indian sub-continent. Archaeological research shows that the practice of yoga originated as early as 1500 BC, although written proof of its existence only dates back to 900 BC.

Hatha yoga developed around 1000 AD and includes physical and breathing exercises that help with flexibility and relaxation. Baby yoga is a fairly new practice based on the age-old tradition. It includes simplified Hatha yoga, coupled with rhythmical movement.

Complementing one another – baby massage and baby yoga

As very young babies are often quickly over-stimulated, massage can gently introduce a baby to positive touch. As the baby develops and grows accustomed to being touched and can accept more stimulating experiences, the energetic and stimulating yoga exercises are a great follow-on from the massage.

The massage routine is made up of several strokes for different areas of your baby's body. You are advised to learn one set of strokes for a particular body area per week, for instance, the legs. This gives you the opportunity to become comfortable with how to do the strokes and also allows your baby to become used to massage gradually, if the strokes are practised every day throughout the week. The following week, new strokes for a new area are introduced, whilst also consolidating the strokes from the previous week. This allows for ample practice week by week. Once all the strokes in the routine have been introduced you should feel confident to give your baby the full body massage.

When your baby is comfortable with the full massage routine, this is a good time to introduce them to the yoga exercises. By then, your baby should already be familiar with many aspects that are shared by both massage and yoga. Both give you the opportunity to:

- use positive touch with your baby
- do exercises with your baby

- have special hugs and holds
- use nursery rhymes and music
- spend special time together
- learn about your baby
- relax with your baby
- play with your baby
- have fun together!

Once both the massage and yoga routines have been learnt, you will be able to decide which routine best suits you and your baby on that particular day.

Positive touch for babies

In this day and age, when there are so many gismos and gadgets to help parents to care for their babies (particularly those that help transport babies around), babies are often manoeuvred from their cot to carry-cot to pushchair and then their car seat and it is not uncommon for a baby to be barely touched at all. This is rather unfortunate for a baby who has, until only a short while before, spent nine months inside the confines of the womb in constant touch with their mum. Once born, there are no more cosy walls and gone is the continual massage received whilst mum moved around.

Touch is often not sufficiently considered until we can see the profound effects that little or no touch has on a child. Reports in the last century of babies and children who were deprived of touch in orphanages around the world, show us how important positive touch is to the human race.

Throughout life, no matter what the age, being held and comforted are the most healing acts that humans can share. Without realising, parents instinctively use touch to heal and comfort their children. 'Rub it better' is a phrase very often used to reassure a wounded child – to stroke the area of the skin that has been affected is an instinctive reaction, which encourages our body to start the natural repair process.

Touch is therefore a fundamental need for everybody, but 'skin-to-skin' contact is essential for a newborn baby. It can help with temperature control, stabilising breathing and heart rate, and increases the well-being of the baby. The inclination to ignore the need for skin-to-skin contact between the mother and baby, which is so common in western societies, may affect the ability of the mother to recognize the non-verbal cues or signs through which the baby is trying to communicate.

A parent's ability to understand their baby's cues can be greatly enhanced through baby massage and yoga, allowing the parent to comfort and reassure their baby through positive touch.

> **I like not only to be loved, but to be told I am loved.**
>
> *George Eliot*

02

the benefits of massage and yoga for your baby (and you)

In this chapter you will learn:
- how baby massage helps post-natal illness
- why babies need touch
- how to use massage and yoga to alleviate colic
- how massage and yoga may help your baby sleep.

Why massage and yoga are good for your baby and you

Emotional benefits

When the subjects of baby massage and yoga are discussed, it is often the physical benefits that are considered first, but there are also a number of emotional benefits to be gained by both the baby AND the parent when they engage in baby massage and yoga on a regular basis.

Helping your baby adapt to their new environment

Upon leaving the comfort of their mother's womb, a newborn can find that entering the new phase of their life is rather stressful. Massage and yoga, however, can reduce stress; which is as important for tiny babies as it is for adults! Regular massage can help babies adapt to their new environment and reassure them. In time, when they feel anxious, out of sorts or in a stressful situation, parents can use massage, which their baby recognizes as a pleasant experience, to help calm and soothe their baby. Studies carried out at the Touch Research Institute in Miami showed that Cortisol levels (a hormone we all secrete when we are under stress) were greatly reduced in babies that had a massage to soothe them rather than those that were simply rocked.

Overcoming intrusive medical intervention

Massage and yoga can help babies that have received intrusive medical interventions and may associate touch with a negative experience. If your baby has received some medical intervention, you might find initially that massage and yoga may be far too stimulating and distressing for your baby, but you can overcome this by gently introducing the concept of positive touch to them. This can simply be stroking over your baby's clothes, whilst holding them securely and talking to them soothingly or practising the containment and holding techniques (see Chapter 6).

The length of time it takes for a baby to become comfortable with touch depends upon the nature of the baby and the type of intervention they received. Gradually you will be able to progress to the massage routine and then the yoga exercises (see Chapters 8–18); being guided by your baby's subtle forms of communication (see 'Understanding what your baby is telling you' in Chapter 3). Eventually your baby will gradually begin to associate touch in a positive light and the negative feelings connected with the medical intervention will become a distant memory.

Understanding your baby

Not all parents are completely confident about handling their baby in the first months of their life, which can leave the parents feeling rather inadequate and disempowered. The massage and yoga routines (Chapters 8–18) are designed to help parents feel more confident about touching and handling their babies.

Through massage and yoga you can learn how your baby communicates with you by understanding their positive and negative cues (see Chapter 3). These are the noises, movements and subtle physical changes that your baby makes. This may help you to feel more in control as you gain a greater understanding of your baby and you will find that this enhances the mutual respect between you.

Also, with this greater understanding, the communication between both of you should improve so that you are able to recognize when your baby is over-stimulated, why your baby cries, how to help them become calmer and begin to help your baby use their own self-calming techniques (see Chapter 6).

Bonding with your baby

Touch, eye contact, smell and sounds of the parent's voice are all elements of the bonding process between parent and baby. However, because of the pressures to return to work soon after birth, there is a need for parents and babies to become less dependent upon each other very quickly. Also, spending time holding, touching and chatting to our babies happens less frequently and because of this the bonding process may be affected.

The eminent child psychologist, Bernard Brazelton, believes that touch is central to the development of the bonding relationship between a mother and her baby. Baby massage and yoga are excellent forms of positive touch and therefore, without doubt, are extremely important tools for you to use to help you communicate with your baby; in turn this naturally helps with the attachment and bonding between you.

Case study

'I breastfed my baby for five months and was very proud of myself, having overcome many initial problems with the baby not fixing properly in the early days and suffering from cracked, sore and bleeding nipples. During these five months, I enjoyed breastfeeding and the closeness we shared. I felt we'd bonded well and I put this down to the breastfeeding. However, after five months I really felt that I wanted to give up feeding myself – I had only been feeding my baby from my right breast for three months and the long-term physical effects of this were worrying me. And of course, there was the nagging decision about whether I was going back to work or not.

Finally, after much deliberation I decided I'd done my bit and weaned my baby on to formula milk, but I was missing the closeness that breastfeeding gave us. Around the same time as this we started baby massage and it was brilliant. Apart from all the physical benefits of baby massage, we spent quality time together and maintained the closeness we had when I was breastfeeding.'

Sibling rivalry

When a new baby arrives into a family that already has one or more children, the family dynamics can be changed dramatically. Older siblings can feel alienated, neglected and just down-right jealous of the new arrival. Parents who are sensitive to this know the importance of helping the older children come to terms with and accept the new baby. Baby massage and yoga can be extremely useful in this process.

If you have older children, you can really help make a difference to the way they feel about your new baby by involving them in the routines, thereby showing them that they are still just as important to you as they always were. Not only that, they may enjoy the new found responsibility as 'older' brother or sister.

They can help by:

- preparing the room
- choosing the music and the nursery rhymes
- holding the bottle of oil
- watching for the baby's cues (helping them learn what the baby is saying).

> **Activity**
> A fun idea is to encourage the older child to copy the massage strokes and the yoga exercises, that you are doing with their new brother or sister, on their favourite doll or teddy.

Post-natal illness (depression)

Post-natal illness (PNI) is quite common (up to as many as 20 percent of women experience PNI after the birth of their child) and unfortunately, is often under-recognized and under-treated. PNI usually appears in the early months after childbirth but can occur at any time during the first year of the baby's life. If undetected, a mother may be suffering well beyond this period.

Support and treatment for PNI

If a mother is suffering from PNI it is extremely important that she confides in someone that she trusts, be that her partner, family member, Health Visitor or GP. Attending a post-natal group or baby massage and/or yoga class can be of real benefit as these are very supportive, non-judgemental and usually available in the local community. Often, having the opportunity to share fears and anxiety with other mothers can bring tremendous relief.

Other treatments of post-natal illness include self-help strategies, complementary therapies, counselling, medication/therapy and sometimes hospital-based care.

Evidence that baby massage helps PNI sufferers

It is thought that kissing, cuddling and prolonged gazing at the baby are indicators of a developing bond. Baby massage can ensure that a mother spends quality time with her baby and will help with the bonding process, thus helping the baby to develop a strong attachment to its mother, which can promote a sense of security in the baby. The child is then more likely to grow up self-assured and self-confident.

Unfortunately the bonding and attachment process between a mother and her baby can be greatly impeded, and in some cases it may not happen at all, when a mother is suffering from PNI. Very often mothers who are suffering from PNI avoid eye contact with other people and often avoid communicating generally. Sadly, this can also be the case with her baby.

However, it is proven that baby massage can help break the cycle of negative or limited interaction between a mother and her baby and is a highly effective way of helping mothers that are suffering emotionally. Although there is no official research to indicate that yoga is beneficial in relation to PNI, as the yoga routine encourages interaction, it can be assumed that it is valuable for improving communication and ultimately enhancing the development of a loving, caring, mother–child relationship, just as massage is shown to be.

Mothers suffering from PNI benefit greatly from participating in baby massage on a very regular basis for the following reasons:

• Baby massage can help stimulate an increase in the hormone responsible for maternal feelings.
• The baby is more relaxed, happier and the cycle of negative interaction between mother and baby can be broken.
• Babies who received massage (rather than being rocked) gained more weight.
• Babies who were massaged had less sleep problems.
• Babies are calmer.
• Babies interact better with their mother.
• The mother's stress hormone levels were lower.
• The mother's 'feel good' hormones were increased.

Proof that babies need touch

When studied, baby monkeys:

• prefer a surrogate mum that is warm and cuddly but does not offer food
• ignore a surrogate mum that offers food but is not warm and cuddly.

In short – baby massage has the most profound effect on reducing post-natal illness.

Fathers

The emotional benefits of baby massage, such as quality, one-to-one loving touch, can also be experienced by fathers too. Studies show us that fathers that gave their babies a 15-minute daily massage prior to bedtime for one month, revealed that they communicated much better with their babies.

Physical benefits

Strengthens body systems

Regular massage and yoga may help to strengthen your baby's immune system and increase their resistance to infection. It may also improve blood circulation and help to drain the lymphatic system as well as improving the overall condition of their skin (provided a non-contaminated, organic vegetable oil is applied).

Massaging your baby's face can alleviate nasal congestion and help drain mucus from the nasal passages, which is extremely helpful for when your baby has a snuffle. Also, the Toe Rolling exercise (see Chapter 9) is excellent for helping to alleviate the symptoms of a cold and teething niggles, as this exercise is based around the traditional art of reflexology and the toes represent the face, including the nose, mouth, eyes and sinuses. Not only does massaging your baby's toes alleviate these symptoms, but it also has an immediate effect on their nervous system and encourages general well-being.

Colic

It can be a most upsetting experience for a parent to watch a young baby screaming in agony with, what looks like, severe tummy pains. It often lasts for many hours and usually starts around the same time each day. The condition is harmless, although it can be distressing for a baby to experience and for the parents to observe. This distressing condition often creates stress and anxiety within the home. Parents and other family members may find it difficult to cope with the constant crying, so it's important to seek support and if possible to take a break occasionally.

What is colic?

Colic is uncontrollable, extended crying in a baby who is otherwise healthy and well-fed. Every baby cries, but babies who cry for more than three hours a day, three to four days a week, may have colic. It can start when a baby is around two to four weeks of age and may last for three months, or possibly longer. There are some practitioners who believe that colic does not exist, but for those parents that experience the early evening bouts of screaming and obvious distress with their babies it is definitely real enough! However, colic is not a serious condition.

What causes colic?

The cause of colic is not really known. It is often thought to be related to the digestive system. Another possible cause is a combination of a baby's temperament and an immature nervous system. A baby's temperament may make them highly sensitive to the environment, and they may react to normal stimulation, changes to the environment or pick up on parental stress by crying. A baby is unable to regulate crying once they start because of their immature nervous system.

What are the symptoms?

The main symptom is continuous crying for long periods of time. A baby may look uncomfortable or appear to be in pain and may lift their head, draw their legs up to their tummy, become red in the face and pass wind. Some babies refuse to eat during a colicky bout, though research shows that babies with colic generally continue to eat and gain weight normally.

Although this crying can occur at any time, it usually worsens between 4 p.m. and 8 p.m. – often a time when there is a lot of external stimulation in the home; perhaps older siblings are arriving home from school, the television goes on, the telephone may ring, other family members are arriving home from work, the evening meal is being prepared and the baby, very often, is in the middle of this commotion. Some babies will love the hustle and bustle, but others may hate it, especially those that are sensitive and suffering from colic. It might be expedient to reduce as much of the external stimulations for the baby as possible.

When to see a doctor

Colic does not need medical treatment. However, if you are worried about your baby's crying, you may want to seek advice from a healthcare professional to make sure there is no serious underlying problem. Before visiting a doctor, all other possible causes of crying should be eliminated. These include the following:

- Hunger.
- Tiredness.
- Lack of contact – some babies want to be cuddled all the time.
- Startling e.g. due to a jerky movement or sudden noise.
- Undressing – some babies do not like to be naked.
- Temperature – is your baby too hot or too cold?

- Pain – is there an identifiable source of pain, e.g. a nappy rash or some irritation in clothing?

Using massage and yoga to alleviate colic

Massaging your baby's tummy is a fantastic way to help regulate and strengthen the digestive system and alleviate wind, constipation and colic. It is very important to follow the guide in this book and massage their tummy in a clock-wise direction as this is the direction in which the contents of the bowel move. By doing this you can help to move wind and faeces in the right direction. Furthermore, as massage and yoga can be relaxing, a stressed baby may find they are less anxious.

However, it is extremely important that you do not massage your baby whilst they are crying with pain. Firstly, crying is a 'negative cue' (see Chapter 3) and a parent would not be listening to their baby if they ignored this and started to massage their tummy, regardless. Secondly, the best way to alleviate the problem is to catch it early before the baby is in real pain. Parents with a colicky baby will know the signs and the usual time that their baby will begin to suffer with colic – which is so often around tea time.

Using the colic routine

- A simple colic routine has been included in Chapter 10 and when followed and repeated preferably three or four times an hour before the time the colic begins, you should see a marked difference in your baby.
- After the colic routine, allow your baby to rest quietly.
- Your baby may find it particularly calming when facing a blank wall for a little while (especially if there is much commotion in the home).
- The Lazy Lion Containment Hold (see Chapter 6) is extremely good for alleviating the discomfort of stomach ache and colic.

Other treatments for colic

There is no single cure for colic, but there are several measures that can be taken that may help. Individual babies have different needs, and parents should try various methods to see what works.

Parents who bottle-feed their babies may want to try a different formula. For mothers who breastfeed, it is a good idea to continue this because weaning the baby from breast milk may make the colic worse.

Some nursing mothers find that certain foods in their diet seem to worsen the effects of colic so cutting these foods out can help. These might include cruciferous vegetables (e.g. cabbage, broccoli, cauliflower, sprouts and parsnip), beans, onions, garlic, apricots, melon, spicy foods, caffeine and alcohol.

If there is a family history of milk sugar (lactose) intolerance, breastfeeding mothers could try eliminating cows milk from their diet (however, seek advice before making major changes to any diet). Sometimes babies are not able to digest lactose well – this improves as they get older.

If your baby seems to have a lot of wind, make sure they are winded after each feed. Babies who are bottle-fed may swallow air from the bottle; try feeding your baby in a different position, or use a bottle and teat designed to reduce the amount of air your baby swallows during a feed.

Restful sleep

One of the issues, which every new parent has to cope with, is not getting enough sleep. If your baby is finding it difficult to get to sleep, or is waking several times in the night, you will be suffering all the more.

Try not to be drawn into comparisons with other babies. Babies do not know the difference between night and day at first and most babies less than six months wake up regularly during the night. For the first three or four months, babies find it difficult to go more than six hours at night without a feed and this is even truer for breast-fed babies. However, babies may not always wake for hunger. They are emotionally dependent on their parents and will learn from experience that if needed their parent will respond. A baby does not have the capacity to understand anyone else's feelings and if they seem to be very demanding it is not because they are 'trying it on'. A baby that has a feeling of being loved during its first year is more likely to know that a parent will come to them if really needed and not to fret if the attention is not immediate. If the parent responds, the baby's confidence will grow, and eventually they will learn to settle or entertain themselves (see 'Calming techniques' in Chapter 6).

How massage and yoga may help your baby sleep

Many babies find massage very soothing, and may even fall asleep immediately afterwards. You may find that your baby will sleep deeper and longer after a massage. If massage is introduced after their bath and as part of your baby's going-to-bed routine, it can help to release the tension in your baby, not to mention you!

The massage and yoga improves a baby's circulation, deepens and regulates the breathing, and increases the levels of oxygen in the bloodstream, which can lead to deeper sleep. Massage can help to make sleep-time more peaceful with a familiar pattern to it, which is very beneficial for fussy babies.

Other tips to help your baby sleep

In addition to using the massage and yoga techniques, try the following:

- Carrying your baby in a front sling or back pack.
- Swaddling your baby to help them feel secure.
- Placing your baby facing a blank wall, away from distractions.
- Placing your baby near continuous noise or vibrations from household appliances like the washing machine, dishwasher or vacuum cleaner.
- Helping your baby to practise their self-calming techniques.

If your baby does not fall asleep in the evening, wakes during the night or early in the morning or cries excessively, then try some of the following:

Sleeping without a teat cue
Your baby *will* learn very quickly that sleep follows a feed. To help your baby fall asleep without the need for a teat or breast in their mouth, it may be worth rousing them a little as you finally put them down to sleep so they feel themselves dozing off without something in their mouth.

Time to settle
Give your baby time to settle, but do not leave him/her crying and distressed for too long. The same applies if your baby wakes in the night.

Sleepy atmosphere
Whisper to your baby very quietly and soothingly so as to create a sleepy atmosphere. This gives them the opportunity to learn that this is different from daytime.

Toys
A lot of older babies become fond of a cuddly toy that has been introduced to them in the cot at an early stage. They will use this

to cuddle before falling asleep. From about five months old, babies often like to play with a small toy during massage. The toy they cuddle at bedtime could be used for this purpose. It is common for children to hang onto this toy when they are ill or visiting new and strange places – it is known as a 'transitional object'. A transitional object is one that your baby associates with you and their lovely massage, from which they can take comfort in your absence.

Warmth

Babies sleep better when they are warm. Babygros can keep them warm when they kick off blankets, but if your baby is very restless then a fitted sleeping blanket might be the answer. Make sure the blanket fits well, has no arms and has a tog rating of no higher than 1.5. (For safe sleeping, babies should not overheat either.)

Light

When attending to your baby in the night, do this in the dark so that your baby does not associate 'lights on' with visits from mummy or daddy! Night lights can help children drift off to sleep (for safety reasons switch these off when you go to bed). Black-out blinds can be useful in summer to cut out the early morning sun.

Noise

A certain amount of low level noise can be comforting for your baby. However, sudden, loud noise can disturb their sleep. If possible, move your baby to another room away from noise. Central heating noise can be a real problem for disturbing sleep. One helpful idea could be to delay the onset in the morning by half an hour so that your baby gets more sleep.

Music

Some babies respond to the rhythmic sounds of music. This works best when the baby is rocked from head to toe (rather than from side to side). Soothing music, or music that was played whilst the baby was still in the womb (in the third trimester) can be have a calming effect once the baby is born.

Natural pain relief

Generally, massage stimulates the production of Oxytocin (a hormone secreted by both sexes), which is a natural pain reliever and induces a calming effect for your baby.

Putting your baby in prone position during the day

A number of weeks prior to learning the back massage strokes, it is advisable that you lay your baby on their tummy for a short period each day. This helps your baby to feel comfortable and gain confidence in this position. Also, it can help with the crawl response and encourages your baby to lift its head. Your baby may resist initially as they may find it strange, so it is always best if you try this for short periods of time to avoid your baby getting tired or irritable.

Activity

In the week leading up to learning the back massage, place your baby on their front for five minutes, a couple of times a day. It is important that this activity is only carried out when you are able to stay with them to reassure them. Remember that this is new to them, and also, from a safety point of view, **your baby should never be left alone at this time.**

The benefits of the prone position

Lying your baby on their tummy is a great way to help with their muscle development and to increase strength. It also helps your baby to be able to:

- feel confident being on their front
- lift their head, to turn and look
- lift their upper body with support from their forearms
- push their arms into a rigid position. (This may cause your baby to roll over so **never leave your baby alone on a raised surface, changing platform or bed**)
- move their weight on to one hand enabling them to reach for a toy
- practise the crawl movement by drawing their knees towards their hips
- push up with their hands when on their knees so they can rock.

Since it has become more popular to put babies on their backs to sleep, this practice has now become an 'all day routine'. This has led to an increase of babies with 'flat head syndrome' or an abnormal shaped head. So, during supervised play time, it will be helpful for your baby's development if they spend time on their tummy.

One session of baby yoga gives enough physical activity that
is equivalent to having been handled and carried all day.

Helping your baby's cognitive development

Cognitive development is the process by which the brain develops the abilities to learn thinking, reasoning, memory and language skills during their early years and helps a child create an impression of the world around them.

These abilities start to develop in early infancy as the brain begins forming connections: during the first two years of life a baby's brain is developing at an exceptional rate. At birth, babies mainly rely on the primitive part of the brain to help them through the early stages of their life. This primitive part of the brain, which functions on a basic instinctual and emotional level only, is not 'wired up' to the front part of the brain that is responsible for rational thoughts. The pathways from the primitive brain to the frontal brain need to connect in the early years to enable a child to grow into a rational, reasoning and caring human being.

To help make these connections, a baby requires lots of positive and varied experiences such as new sights, sounds, smells and tactile stimulation. Massage and yoga are excellent ways of bringing new and positive experiences into a young baby's life as they offer the opportunity for positive touch and early play, especially when accompanied with lots of talking, music and singing of nursery rhymes. Studies show that using nursery rhymes in play can be a wonderful learning tool and can enhance brain development in a growing baby. Other studies have shown that positive experiences (such as baby massage and yoga) in the first two years of a baby's life, enhances not only the physical development of the child but also their brain development. Baby massage and yoga allow a baby to have fun and gives them many positive experiences.

Your baby's cognitive development between 1 and 12 months of age

The brain development follows a typical pattern in the first 12 months of a baby's life:

- Between 1 and 2 months of age, babies become interested in new objects and will turn and look towards them. They also gaze longer at more complicated objects and seem to enjoy looking at many new objects, as though trying to learn as much about their new world as possible.
- At around 3 months of age, babies are able to anticipate future events. For example, they will become excited when their parent gently lays their hands on their chest and asks if they want a massage.
- At around 4 months, a baby's sight becomes more advanced and they are now able to combine what they see with what they taste, hear and feel. A baby will be able to wiggle and feel their fingers, and see their fingers move as they become more self-aware. Massage can help them become more aware of their legs, feet, arms and hands.
- Connections in the brain are growing rapidly between 6 and 9 months of age. Babies can recognize the appearance, sound and touch of familiar people. Also, babies are able to recall the memory of a person, such as a parent, or an object when that particular person or object is not in view.
- At 9 to 12 months of age a baby is constantly observing the behaviour of others. They start to reveal their personality and become curious about their surroundings and begin to explore. They are also able to demonstrate many different emotions. At this curious stage, massage may become more of a challenge as the baby may not want to lie still.

Cognitive development 12–18 months

- Between the ages of 12 to 18 months, toddlers continue to explore their environment and create experiments to see how things work. They will play with anything they can find; however, at this stage they are not aware of danger so they do not realise that certain things like fires, sharp knives and electric plug sockets can hurt them.
- During this stage the ability to recognize people and objects moves on a step – not only do the babies realise that something can be hidden and still exist, but by now they will look for it too.
- Also around this time, babies develop the capacity to build memories that incorporate all their senses. For instance, children are able to see a mental picture of an object they are holding in their hand without actually looking at it. They remember the object as a whole, through all their senses; they

remember its texture and size in their hands, its sound through their ears, and perhaps even its smell.

Cognitive development 18–24 months

- Between the ages of 18 and 24 months, toddlers are able to create a generic image of things in their minds and retain them as examples of certain objects. They may create in their mind a picture of a teddy bear, and use it to represent other cuddly animals they play with. Because of this, babies may look for their favourite teddy bear in the toy box because they know that is where it usually lives!

- At this stage, a baby's recall and recognition memory also improves significantly. Around 21 months old, toddlers learn routines, about how certain things are done. For example, they learn that 'an outing to the park', is 'Mum collects the coats and hats, mum puts on baby's coat and hat, mum puts toddler in the pushchair. Mum opens the front door. Mum and toddler leave the house'. With massage and yoga, you may find that when you ask your baby if they want a massage they will start to collect some of the equipment, such as the bottle of oil, or they may remove some of their clothes and lie on the floor in anticipation!

- Also around 21 months of age, babies reach a number of other developmental milestones and have grasped the concept of past, present and future.

- They also begin to understand that 'things' fit into certain categories, such as recognising a car as a car, even though all cars do not look the same.

- They begin to recognize what things are alike and why, and what other objects fit or do not fit into particular categories.

- Around 24 months of age, toddlers are able to pretend and imagine things that aren't there in front of them. This is the first step beyond 'concrete thinking' which means only being able to think about things that are in front of them. Introducing a simple story-time massage, for instance about a little cat or dog, can help encourage their imagination.

Let's recap

Benefits for baby

Massage and yoga can:

- help a baby adapt to their new environment and become generally more settled
- help a baby develop their first language – touch
- enhance baby's feeling of being loved, respected and secure
- promote relaxation, which can improve quality of sleep
- help a baby cope with stressful situations by regulating Cortisol levels
- reduce the discomfort of colic, wind and constipation
- regulate and strengthen their digestive, respiratory and immune systems
- stimulate the circulatory system and balance the nervous system
- stimulate the lymphatic system
- help general growth and cognitive development
- develop body-mind awareness and coordination
- improve skin condition
- help the baby associate touch with positive handling (particularly important for babies who have experienced intrusive medical intervention)
- strengthen and tone muscles
- help maintain flexibility of the joints, ligaments and tendons
- help the development of coordination, balance and motor skills
- stimulate all the senses
- help a baby learn to interact and play with others.

Benefits for parents

Massage and yoga can:

- help parents to become more confident and competent in handling their baby
- help parents to understand their baby's non-verbal communication
- help parents to relax whilst having fun with their baby
- help develop a feeling of closeness with their baby
- give a time for parents to play constructively with their baby, so that the relationship may strengthen and grow
- encourage lactation through the stimulation of Prolactin
- encourage the nurturing instinct through the stimulation of Oxytocin
- help parents feel more in control
- strengthen a parent's physical health (yoga).

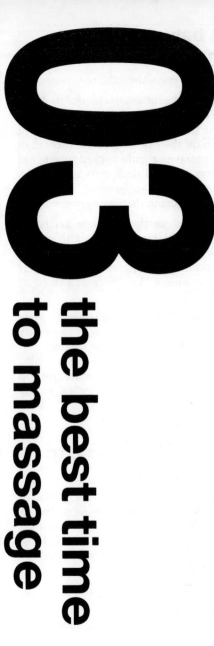

03

the best time to massage

In this chapter you will learn:
- when is the best time to do massage and yoga
- how to understand what your baby is telling you
- whether your baby is saying 'yes' to massage and yoga
- when not to do massage and yoga with your baby.

How old should a baby be before massage and yoga can be introduced?

Positive touch, holding and containment are wonderful tools for parents to use in the first few weeks of their baby's life, when massage and yoga may be far too stimulating for the newborn, particularly as they feel touch on their skin more intensely than an older child (the touch receptors are tightly packed together in the newborn and disperse with age) and their early experiences are multi-sensory (for example, they 'see' sounds and 'hear' colour). Also, they need time to adjust to their new environment.

Generally, a good time to introduce the massage and yoga routines is after a baby has had their six week health check. Although a six week old baby may still be quite sensitive to over-stimulation, they are at least becoming familiar with their surroundings at this stage and are more likely to be able to enjoy massage and yoga.

This doesn't mean that you can't introduce massage to your baby at all during the first few weeks. As massage can greatly help alleviate colic, you may wish to try the colic routine with your baby (see Chapters 2 and 10). The yoga holds are also useful for helping to calm a newborn baby. These are not too stimulating and will give you the opportunity to gently introduce yoga to your young baby (see Chapter 6).

What time of day is the best time to do baby massage and yoga?

Because babies naturally go through six different states of consciousness many times during the day, there will be occasions in the day when your baby will be more receptive to having a massage or doing some yoga exercises. By understanding these states, it becomes easier to anticipate when your baby might be ready to have a massage, or do some yoga.

The six different states of consciousness are as follows:

- A *deep sleep state* is when a baby's eyes are firmly closed: breathing is deep and regular with no arm or leg movement. This is a time when the baby needs to rest as it gives them time to rest and grow.

- A *light sleep state* is when the baby's eyes are firmly closed but eyelid movement can be seen. The baby may twitch a little and their breathing is likely to be irregular and shallow.
- A *drowsy state* is when the baby is just beginning to awaken from their sleep. Their eyes may be open, but with a dazed appearance. There breathing is regular but faster and shallower than when they are asleep.
- An *alert, awake state* is when the baby is relatively quiet and seems able to focus on a person or an object. The sights and sounds around them are likely to produce a response; in this state a baby can be very enjoyable for parents. The baby will be responsive to the voice of its parents and is more likely to respond to singing and having fun during this time. This is a good time to see if a baby is happy to have a massage or do some yoga.
- An *alert, but fussy state* is when a baby is possibly going to cry, but is not actually crying as yet. They may be soothed or brought to a calmer state by an attractive stimulus. If the stimulus is too much, they may become fussy and then start crying. This would not be a good time to start massage or do some yoga if your baby was not used to the routines and did not know how they felt about these activities. However, after a baby has become accustomed to massage and yoga, and understands that they enjoy this time, it might be possible to suggest massage or yoga to a baby whilst in this state, which may help calm them.
- *Crying* is the sixth state and allows a baby the chance to release tension. It is their way of signalling an urgent need. Crying is often a sign that a baby is hungry, in pain, bored, in some discomfort or tired. It is generally the most effective way to get a parent's attention.

Understanding why babies cry

Crying is the way in which babies communicate their distress and their need for attention. Crying is a baby's genuine request for help, and not a way of manipulating its parents to give them undue attention. When crying, a baby is hoping to receive a response from their parent, so that their distress can be alleviated. The uneasy feeling that crying causes a parent is as natural as the crying itself; we are designed to respond to our baby's cry and not to ignore it.

If an adult is ignored they can either raise their voice until they are heard or perhaps rephrase what they have said. However, if they are repeatedly ignored they may give up trying and become withdrawn, feeling quite dejected. Babies react in the same way: if ignored they cry louder, if continually ignored they eventually withdraw into themselves and do not try to communicate how helpless they feel. Eventually they will lower their expectations of care, and of themselves – believing that they are not worthy of more attention.

It can be difficult for parents to understand what their baby is trying to say to them when they are crying, but in time this becomes easier and parents begin to recognize what the different cries mean. There are eight main causes of crying:

- hunger
- tiredness
- pain
- discomfort
- loneliness
- over-stimulation
- under-stimulation
- frustration.

> If your baby's cries for help are consistently met in a sensitive way they will begin to cry less as they learn to trust that you understand and are there to help and comfort them when they need you.

Hunger

If a baby is hungry, the crying will normally stop when they are offered food. If a baby has been left to cry for sometime and has worked itself into a highly emotional state, the baby may need to be calmed before they will accept food. It is important to remember that when a baby experiences the feeling of hunger it happens quickly. It is a sensation that can distress a baby – to them it is a survival instinct.

Tiredness

Many babies cry just before they go to sleep and on waking again. When a baby cries before dropping off to sleep they can feel out of sorts, irritated and often do not want to give in to it.

A baby's sleep cry tells the parent that the baby needs to be helped to go to sleep. This does not necessarily mean that they want to be cuddled to sleep just that they may need assistance in accessing their own ability to self-calm.

Pain

If adults hurt themselves they are often very verbal in their reaction, but it is rare that they resort to crying. A baby is quick to cry with any pain and there is a good reason why. A baby cannot assess how badly it is hurt; it cannot distinguish between a small bruise or a more serious injury. In order to protect themselves, babies cry in order to bring the parent to their aid and so that the cause of their pain can be assessed and the appropriate action taken. A baby's cry of pain is hard to ignore because it tends to be loud, sharp and intense: a baby with colic is a good example.

Discomfort

If a baby is uncomfortable, wet or dirty, they may cry. The cry is milder and lacks the sharpness of the pain cry but is designed so as not to be ignored.

Loneliness

Sometimes a baby will cry if they feel lonely. They may simply want to be close to someone special and have a cuddle. Even the smallest of babies are sociable and want to be with other people who are most familiar to them, in particular their Mum. Parents that take time to be with their baby are helping to make them feel secure and confident. This helps to make them feel loved and believe that they are loveable.

Over-stimulation

Too much light, sound or activity can make a baby cry. Over-stimulation is a form of sensory pain where a baby's eyes, ears or general nervous system are suffering from too much input. Over-powering smells can also trigger a reaction. The situations that we, as adults, have become conditioned to tolerate can be too much for a baby. As able adults we can remove ourselves from an intolerable situation, a baby cannot.

Under-stimulation

Boredom can become a problem with older babies, particularly when they are over six months old. Crying during this stage may be from boredom, so it is important to vary your baby's environment by providing access to colours, shapes, textures and sounds in order to stimulate the senses.

Frustration

This can be a problem with older babies who find their clumsiness or lack of mobility a barrier to reaching their goal. If they try to do something and fail, they may start to cry as a way of getting Mum or Dad's help, so that they can achieve what they wanted to do. For example, a baby may cry with frustration until they master a new skill, such as crawling and walking.

Activity

- Take time to watch your baby so you begin to notice what sort of things they do before they start to cry.
- Take time to listen to your baby so that you begin to notice the different types of cry they make, which will help you become aware of whether they are hungry or tired, etc.

Understanding what your baby is telling you

Your baby will tell you how they are feeling and what they want by using 'non-verbal cues'. There is no 'recipe' of cues – all babies are individual and will have different ways of telling their parents want they want. Sometimes the cues will be very positive and your baby will let you know how happy they are. Other times, your baby will not be happy and will use negative cues to show you how they feel.

Positive cues

When a baby wants to communicate with someone they might:

- be still
- gaze at a face
- reach out to the person

- turn their head and eyes towards the person
- smile
- coo
- use gentle movements of the arms and legs
- have bright, wide open eyes
- look alert and awake, bright and responsive.

Negative cues

When a baby wants a break or a rest they will disengage and withdraw. They might:

- turn away
- cry
- become fussy
- cough
- hiccup
- yawn
- wrinkle their forehead
- arch their back
- fall asleep
- squirm
- kick and pull away
- have mottled skin.

Children in Bali are considered to be angels from heaven. The cultural belief is that they must not be 'shocked by contact with the heaviness of the world' at birth. Therefore, a newborn's feet are not allowed to touch the earth for the first 105 days of their life. The baby is held continually until almost four months of age. Then, during a special ceremony, the baby's feet are placed upon the ground accompanied by prayers and blessings.

Is your baby saying 'yes' to massage and yoga?

When you are deciding whether your baby is saying 'yes' to massage or yoga, it is important to think about their non-verbal cues, so that you can decide if it is a good time for them or not.

Positive cues are more likely to indicate that your baby is saying 'yes' to massage or yoga; and the negative cues are probably a sign that it is not the right time for your baby, and they are saying 'no' to the activity.

Sometimes you might find it difficult to know whether your baby is saying 'yes' or 'no', particularly when their non-verbal cues are quite subtle and if you have not given it any thought before. Do not worry, this understanding will come in time, and you will find that if you have not understood what your baby is saying immediately, they will give out even stronger cues, making it quite clear how they are feeling.

During the massage and yoga routines it is vital that your baby is happy, in order for them to learn that these activities are fun and that when they say 'no' to massage or yoga, they are heard, listened to, and their feelings are respected. If a baby's 'no' cues are ignored, they will believe they do not have a voice and that their feelings are not worthy of attention. Also, babies that are not listened to often become withdrawn and generally less responsive.

You will probably find that when your baby is in an alert, awake state during the day, they are more likely to say 'yes' to massage or yoga, because they are keen to play and have fun with you during these periods. Many babies enjoy a massage just before or after a bath – you might find this also fits in with your routine. However, your baby may become quite excited after massage and in particular yoga, so it may be that first thing in the morning is better for you both. What is important is that it is right for your baby and you, so that massage and yoga are thoroughly enjoyable experiences.

When is it not a good time to do massage and yoga with your baby

It is important to avoid doing massage and yoga with your baby if they:

- are asleep, tired, hungry, crying or fretful, because these are all **'no'** cues
- are unwell, or have a raised temperature. Their immune system will need to be left to deal with the problem and not be over stimulated by massage or yoga

- have an infectious skin condition, because this may aggravate the infected area. The most common skin infections in children are impetigo and ringworm. It is best to refrain from massage and skin-to-skin contact as there is a risk of cross-infection
- are suffering from bruising, sprains or a fracture. It is advisable to refrain from massage until the injuries have healed completely and the swelling has gone down. It may be possible for the unaffected areas to be massaged, but yoga may cause pain and should be avoided until the baby is well again
- have open, weeping wounds and rashes or have an unhealed navel. Breaks in the skin may become infected if massaged and this might cause discomfort and pain
- are suffering from Jaundice, as their liver is most likely not functioning as it should. Refrain from massage and yoga until the liver is functioning correctly
- have received vaccinations within the previous three days. Vaccinations have an impact on the immune system, as vaccines trigger the immune system to produce antibodies in a similar manner to that of the actual disease. Because massage and yoga are stimulating and have an impact on the immune system, it is necessary to have a break from these activities, so that your baby's body is not overloaded or over-stimulated whilst it is trying to deal with the vaccinations given
- have been diagnosed with brittle bone disease. The bones in children suffering from this disease can be so brittle that they break with normal handling.

It is advisable to check with your baby's GP or consultant, before commencing massage and yoga, if your baby has any medical conditions and/or has undergone recent surgery. Generally, after surgery, refrain from massaging the affected area for at least eight weeks to allow the wound to heal. However other areas of your baby's body could be massaged once they have recovered from having an operation. Only massage the unaffected areas once your baby has been given the all clear by the surgeon or GP. It is advisable to avoid yoga until the wound is completely healed. As yoga is quite dynamic, the wound may be affected by many of the exercises.

Summary

The best time to do massage and yoga with your baby is when your baby is in an alert and awake state.

When your baby is relatively quiet, with bright shining eyes, is interested in the sights and sounds around them and is able to focus on you, they are likely to be in an alert, awake state. These are the times when they are more likely to be responsive to your voice; try chatting, singing and having fun during this time.

Another good time to do massage and yoga is when your baby is showing positive cues, such as:

- staying still
- gazing at your face
- reaching out to you
- turning their head and eyes towards you
- smiling
- cooing
- gently moving their arms and legs
- opening their eyes, bright and wide
- looking alert and awake, bright and responsive.

During the times when your baby is in an alert, awake state and displaying positive cues, you will find that they are likely to be responsive to receiving a massage or doing some yoga.

04

preparing for massage and yoga

In this chapter you will learn:
- how to prepare the equipment and room for massage
- how to prepare the equipment and room for yoga
- how to prepare yourself for the massage and yoga
- relaxation techniques.

Preparing the environment for massage and yoga

There is nothing very complicated about preparing for baby massage and yoga and it doesn't cost the earth. Before any massage begins it is important to make sure that the environment is just right to create a peaceful atmosphere so that the experience is as relaxing as possible. The same applies with baby yoga too. The space will need to be comfortable, quiet and somewhere that will have few distractions. Not only will you need to prepare the space around you, but you will also need to prepare yourself physically (such as wearing comfortable clothing) and mentally (such as finding time within your busy schedule). These things will ensure that the massage is a positive experience for both your baby and you.

Preparing for massage

The room

- **Warmth:** Choose a room that will be warm enough to undress your baby in and that they will be comfortable when naked; although make sure it is not so warm that they become hot and sweaty during the massage. If you feel comfortably warm in a short-sleeved top then this is a good indicator.

- **Light:** Be aware of your environment and use natural daylight, where possible. If this is not possible, introduce soft, subtle lighting such as a lamp to create a warm, relaxing atmosphere. Your baby, for the most part, will be lying on their backs giving them the opportunity to look at you and the ceiling. Bright lights can be very distracting for your baby. If a main light has to be used then make sure your baby is not directly beneath it.

- **Noise:** Try to ensure the room is as quiet as possible and that external noises and distractions are kept to a minimum. It is a good idea to turn off televisions, radios, loud household machines, mobile phones and remove noisy, boisterous pets!

- **Music:** Introducing soothing music can really help to create a relaxing atmosphere for both you and your baby. You should be careful to select music that is not too stimulating for the massage routine. Instruments are the voice of music and traditional instruments, which produce musical notes by natural means, are the most relaxing, for example, flutes, strings and harps, rather than synthesized sounds which can be too much for a baby's delicate ears and sensitive nervous system. Try to select melodies and lullabies with a calming tempo. For recommended music please see the Taking it further section.

- **Smells:** One of the wonderful benefits of massaging your baby is that you both have a special time to spend together which can greatly strengthen your bond. Part of the bonding process is a baby becoming familiar with its parent's natural smell and vice versa. Try to eliminate any artificial smells such as perfumes, air fresheners or aromatherapy oils. It is important to remember, just because you like a particular fragrance it does not necessarily mean that your baby does too! In fact it could irritate and become very distracting for your baby.

Equipment

Before the massage begins, prepare the following items:

- Changing mat or large thick towel for your baby to lie on.
- Large towel rolled up into a sausage that can be used for containment of a smaller baby or used for alternative positions for the back massage.
- CD player and relaxing music.
- A pillow for you to sit on or to be used for alternative positions.
- Tissues, baby wipes or a spare towel for little accidents!
- Small bottle or dish of massage oil at room temperature.
- Teddy or toy and a small mirror to amuse older babies.
- Fresh nappy for when the massage is complete.
- A drink for your baby to have when the massage is over.
- This book!

Preparing for yoga

The room

- **Space:** Choose a room that is carpeted and spacious enough so that you and your baby can move about safely and with ease. Ensure pets are not going to get under foot.
- **Warmth:** Choose a room that is warm but not too hot – your baby does not need to be undressed during the exercises and may over-heat.

- **Light:** Choose a room that is light and airy. As there is some floor work, make sure your baby is not directly beneath an artificial ceiling light, as this can be distracting.
- **Music:** Soothing background music can really help to create a relaxing atmosphere.

Equipment

Before the yoga routine, prepare the following items:

- Yoga mat or non-slip rug for floor exercises.
- CD player and relaxing music.
- A pillow for you to sit on.
- A drink of water for you and your baby to have afterwards.
- This book!

Getting your baby ready for massage and yoga

Refer to Chapter 3, 'The best time to massage'.

Getting yourself ready for massage and yoga

Not only do you need to prepare the room, the equipment and your baby, but *you* need to be prepared too. It is vital to be as relaxed as possible before giving your baby a massage or starting the yoga session. Sometimes, this is easier said than done! So, do try the relaxation techniques below; they may be helpful.

- **Be comfortable:** It is advisable to wear comfortable clothing, as you will be spending lots of time sitting on the floor when massaging and moving around for the yoga exercises. Wearing a t-shirt or loose top may allow for easier movement and ensures that you do not become too warm. Use a cushion or pillow to sit on to reduce any discomfort for floor work.
- **Jewellery:** Remove any jewellery that may scratch your baby's skin or dangle in their face.
- **Hands and nails:** Ensure that your hands are washed before the massage and any nail snags have been filed away. Take care to use only the pads of your fingers when massaging your baby, as long nails, in particular, may cause discomfort to the baby if they dig into their skin.

- **Hair:** If you have long hair it is advisable to have it tied back during the massage and yoga, this will ensure it does not dangle on your baby's skin and tickle.
- **Position:** You need to be aware of your sitting position so that you are comfortable when doing the floor exercises and massage routine. Use a cushion or beanbag and, if possible, rest against a wall, or a sturdy piece of furniture.
- **Relaxation techniques:** It is important before starting the massage or yoga that you feel as **relaxed** as possible and have put the worries of the day behind you for the time being.

Relaxation techniques for you to try

If you are not relaxed, your baby will intuitively feel it during the routines and will not benefit as much as they could do. Possibly, they may refuse the massage or the yoga session altogether because of the tension they sense in you. (It is recommended that you try these relaxation techniques at any time of the day if you feel tense, regardless of whether you are about to massage your baby or not.)

A short relaxation technique

- Sit in a comfortable position (if this is just before the massage or yoga, hold your baby or place your hands gently on them whilst your baby is lying on the mat).
- Close your eyes.
- Inhale deeply and slowly through your nose, filling the whole of your lungs.
- Exhale slowly through your mouth.
- Repeat three times.
- During the breathing exercise, consciously relax tense areas, such as neck, shoulders, back and upper arms.
- Imagine a bright golden light shining above you.
- Whilst you are breathing in, imagine the bright light being drawn into your body through your head all the way down to the end of your fingers and toes.
- Imagine this glorious light filling the whole of your body with calm and peace.
- Whilst exhaling, think of the word 'CALM'.
- Repeat three times.
- Now focus on your baby.

- Slowly open your eyes.
- Once you are relaxed, massage and yoga can begin. If not, repeat the above.

A deep relaxation technique

For parents who have problems relaxing, try the deeper relaxation technique below. It is advisable that this is done when your baby is asleep or being cared for by someone else.

- Lie in a comfortable position.
- Inhale deeply and slowly.
- Exhale slowly through your mouth.
- Repeat three times.
- SLOWLY
  - tense your toes, relax your toes
  - tense your ankles, relax your ankles
  - tense your calves, relax your calves
  - tense your knees, relax your knees
  - tense your thighs, relax your thighs
  - tense your buttocks, relax your buttocks
  - tense your abdomen, relax your abdomen
  - tense your chest, relax your chest
  - tense your back, relax your back
  - tense your arms and hands, relax your arms and hands
  - tense your shoulders, relax your shoulders
  - tense your neck, relax your neck
  - tense your face, relax your face
  - tense your head, relax your head.
- Imagine your are in a beautiful place somewhere in nature, a very special place.
- Imagine the sun high above your head in a beautiful blue sky.
- Lie in this beautiful place for as long you need.
- When you are ready, slowly come to the present.
- When ready, slowly open your eyes.
- Stretch out the whole of your body.
- When ready, sit up slowly.

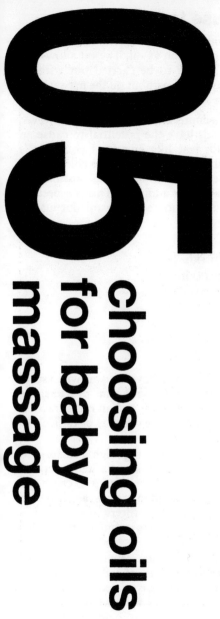

05
choosing oils for baby massage

In this chapter you will learn:
- which oils are best for baby massage
- which oils to avoid
- where to buy oils
- how to store oils safely.

The best oils to use for massage

For massage to be enjoyable and comfortable for your baby it is best to use a massage medium, such as oil. The oil allows the massage movements and strokes to be carried out without causing friction to your baby's skin; without oil the massage can be irritating, especially for a sensitive newborn.

Plant-based oils are ideal mediums for baby massage; however, care needs to be taken as oils have the potential to cause an allergic reaction in a child, just like any food could. It is recommended, where possible, that an organic or cold-pressed vegetable oil is used because they are as natural as possible and contain little or no preservatives or additives. This is especially important as babies may ingest some of the oil during the massage. Natural vegetable oils:

- allow the skin to breathe
- nourish and moisturise the skin
- are easily absorbed into the skin
- are unscented
- are natural and safe.

Vegetable oils

- **Organic oil** that is truly organic will have been grown in strict organic conditions; starting with the seed, nuts or fruits; the condition of soil; no use of pesticides; and an oil extraction process that is free of chemicals. These oils may be difficult to find and can be expensive.
- **Cold-pressed oil** is produced by using high pressure to squeeze out the oil from soft, oily seeds such as Sunflower and Olive. For harder seeds, more pressure is used to crush the seed, which generates some heat (and may alter the oil). After crushing, the shells are removed by filters and the oil is natural. (Some oils may be further refined after cold-pressing.)
- **Refined oils** The vegetable pulp that remains after cold-pressing still contains some oil and is refined either by high temperatures, high pressures or may be treated with steam or solvents. This process alters the oil somewhat to remove allergens and impurities, which can help to make it hypoallergenic and safer to use with babies that are prone to allergic reactions or who have weaker immune systems.

What to choose?

Parents will have a number of reasons for choosing a particular oil, but careful consideration should be given to:

- availability
- the skin type of your baby
- risk of allergic reactions
- how the oil will be stored.

Sunflower oil (*Helianthus annuus*)

Sunflower oil is excellent for baby massage; it has a light texture and does not leave the skin feeling greasy. The oil is made from the seed of the plant and closely resembles Sebum (the oil that is already present in the human skin) and therefore the sunflower oil is easily absorbed by the uppermost layers of the skin. As the oil is rather light, it can be used to dilute a heavier oil, such as olive oil. This oil produces few allergic reactions, but those people that are allergic to sunflower seeds should avoid cold-pressed and refined sunflower oils. Organic and cold-pressed are best for use with baby massage but refined oils (food grade) are also possible alternatives.

Olive oil (*Olea europaea*)

This oil, produced from the flesh of the olive, is rather heavy and viscous and may stain clothing, it can however be diluted with sunflower or grape seed oil. Some varieties can have a strong odour too. It is said to have anti-inflammatory properties and can help with sensitive, chapped skin, burns, stings and even nettle rashes! Olive oil is an all-round general emollient. Again, it is recommended that organic, cold-pressed oil is used.

Grape seed oil (*Vitis vinifera*)

This oil is made from the hard stone of the grape and is highly refined due to the manufacture process and has little odour, keeps well, is good for slippage and isn't too greasy when applied to the skin. Depending upon the type of refinement process, this oil is said to be hypoallergenic and therefore good for babies who are prone to allergic reactions and have weak immune systems.

Coconut oil (*Cocos nucifera*)

Coconut oil is made from the flesh of the coconut and in its raw state is a solid, thick fat and very good for skin. For babies who have poor immune systems and nut allergy problems it is not advisable to use this oil (it may also contribute to a child becoming allergic).

However, **fractionated coconut oil** is a refined oil that has been produced from the original solid fat coconut oil being heat treated. The fractionisation of the oil removes all potential allergens, mould spores and impurities leaving pure, perfume-free oil that remains as a liquid. This oil will not go off as quickly as other oils and is excellent for slippage in baby massage.

Nut oils

Nut oils, such as almond and peanut, are generally not recommended for baby massage. The Anaphylaxis Campaign suggests that peanut is a high allergy risk in the UK.

Cooking oils

Cooking oils such as sunflower and grape seed purchased from a supermarket are highly-refined oils (food grade). They have been purified to enable them to have consistent colour and a longer shelf-life.

Caution:

Avoid nut-based and wheat-based oils such as sweet almond, peanut and wheat germ oil as these may contribute to or cause an allergic reaction.

Oils to avoid

Mineral oils

There are a number of mineral oils and commercially available 'baby massage oils or gels' on the market but it is recommended that these are not used for baby massage. Mineral oil/gel is a highly processed by-product of petroleum (paraffin wax). It contains chemicals and preservatives and is **not** broken down by the body's digestive system. It has already been mentioned that oil may be ingested by the baby during massage as oil may be on their hands. Unlike vegetable oil, mineral oil is not absorbed into the outer layers of the skin (the epidermis), therefore creating a barrier of film on the surface of the baby's skin. This can block pores and impede the natural functions of the skin, such as excretion and heat regulation. It does not really offer any benefit to the skin, however it is cheap to mass produce and does not go off.

Artificially scented oil

Some commercial baby massage oils and gels often contain artificial perfumes. It is important to avoid these particular oils because they may contain chemicals that may be harmful when ingested. As the artificial scents are often quite a strong smell, your baby may find them overpowering and over-stimulating for the senses. Furthermore, the scent prevents the baby from smelling their parent's natural scent.

Essential oils

Since the popularity of Aromatherapy, many products containing various essential oils are appearing on the market. Essential oils work in very subtle ways, with very small amounts giving therapeutic effects; some of the oils being the antidote to homeopathic remedies. Indeed, some of the stronger essential oils are so potent when blended that they are capable of eradicating a strain of the life-threatening bug MRSA! Even the oils that are considered to be a softer option, such as lavender and tea tree, are not safe to use on prepubescent children as it has been proven that the hormonal activities in the oil may trigger abnormal breast development in young children.

The chemical content of essential oils is absorbed into the body via the olfactory system (nose and lungs) and 60 per cent of substances massaged in to the skin are absorbed into the blood stream. The molecular structure of essential oil is much smaller than vegetable oil and is therefore able to penetrate through the skin.

Many products on the market, intended for babies, contain a number of essential oils. It is not uncommon to find a whole array of baby products for the bath, the hair, massage gel, nappy rash, oils to burn for inhalation etc., all containing different essential oils claiming to help relax or soothe a baby. If a parent uses all these products on their young baby they could be unwittingly overwhelming their baby's sensitive systems.

Reasons for not using essential oils with children under twelve years of age

- The immune system of a baby is very immature and over-use of essential oils may overwhelm an immature liver and the nervous system.
- To-date there is NO research to validate that the use of essential oils with infants is indeed safe.
- Just because a parent likes the fragrance of a particular oil does not mean that their baby will. Obviously a baby cannot communicate this to their parents.
- The essential oil that is added could mask the odour of a rancid vegetable oil.
- The fragrance added to the oil masks the natural smell of the parent. It is very important for the baby to smell their parent's natural smell which helps with bonding.
- Hormonal activities present them as an unwise choice.

For children over the age of two, those parents wishing to introduce essential oils as a treatment are advised to consult a qualified and registered Aromatherapist who specialises in treating children and their individual needs.

Where to buy oil

- Where possible, buy massage oil from a reputable supplier.
- If buying a vegetable oil from a supermarket, look for organic cold-pressed varieties.

Storage of oils

- It is best to buy organic and cold-pressed vegetable oils in small quantities, as the shelf life is limited (a 50 ml bottle should last several massage sessions).
- Store oils in a cool, dark place such as a larder.
- Leave the oil to warm to room temperature before massage.

- Discard oil that has gone rancid (oil that has gone off has a rather unpleasant odour).
- Do not use old oil that has been left for a while as the air in the bottle will oxidise the oil and it may become rancid.
- Discard any oil that has been decanted into a dish for a massage session. **Do not** return unused oil back into the original bottle as this could potentially contaminate the oil with bacteria.

Rather than using a large bottle of oil for massage, consider decanting some of the oil into a smaller, manageable bottle, or place some oil in a clean, shallow bowl, but remember to discard any left-overs after the massage.

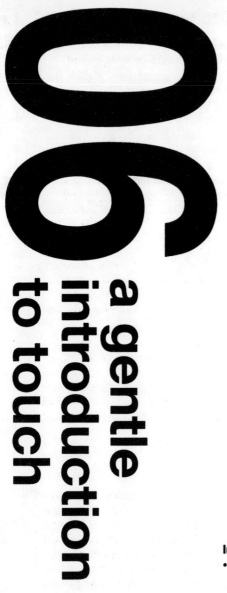

06

a gentle introduction to touch

In this chapter you will learn:
- how to introduce touch and massage to your newborn baby
- holding and containment to help your baby feel secure
- calming techniques to use with your baby.

Introducing touch to your baby

Massage and yoga routines can be fun and are a great way for you to spend time with your baby; but sometimes the full routines can be too stimulating, particularly for the newborn. However, your baby's need to be touched and to feel secure is still important, and there are other ways of introducing touch before you start the massage and yoga.

Holding and containment to help your baby feel secure

Today, with so many baby carriers, such as car seats that also double as pushchairs, a baby's need to be held is easily overlooked. Your baby has lived the first nine months of their life in the warm, safe, confined space of the womb. During this time, they are able to float effortlessly; moving, kicking and stretching, completely protected and safe. By the end of the nine month period the womb becomes very confined, limiting a baby's movement and giving them the greatest sense of containment. A baby's next experience is that of a big, wide world – with lots of open space to deal with.

When a newborn baby is held in someone's arms they are able to maintain a more natural foetal position – their legs are bent at the knee and held towards their body, and their arms are in much the same position, giving them the sense of security that they experienced before birth. This position is lost when the baby is placed in a cot, or car seat, or on a changing mat – along with their sense of security.

Case study

'When Edward was first born and I put him in his cot, whenever I checked him I found that he had wedged himself up against the top of the cot. I thought this would be hurting his head, so I would gently move him down a bit. When Edward was eight weeks old I started to go to baby massage classes and the teacher talked about a baby's need for containment. It was then I realised that that was what Edward was doing – he was trying to make himself feel secure.'

Swaddling

The steady pressure when swaddled gives a baby the feeling of security and comfort that they felt in the womb. Sheets and blankets draped over them and tucked in at the sides of a pram or cot just do not offer the same level of comfort. However, not all babies want to be swaddled, but many do.

Swaddling can:

- be relaxing for a baby
- reduce startling
- reduce crying
- possibly lower the heart rate of a fractious baby.

Activity

If you find that your baby does not settle when you put them in their cot or pram, when they are clearly in need of a sleep, try swaddling them in a very thin cotton blanket or flannelette cot sheet. It is important not to cover their face, and also allow them access to their own hands, in case they want to suck them.

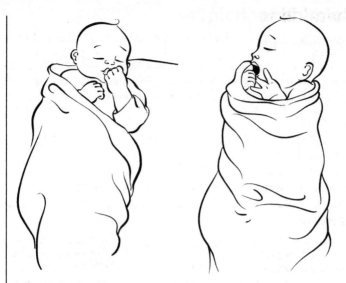

Figure 6.1 Swaddling

How to swaddle your baby

- Place the sheet on a flat surface and fold down the top right corner about 15 cm so the sheet is a triangle.
- Place your baby on the sheet on their back with their head just above the fold.
- Gently support their hands up towards their chin so they can get them to their mouth, if they wish to.
- Pull the corner near your baby's left hand across their body, and tuck this around their right elbow and secure it under their back.
- Pull the bottom corner by their feet up towards your baby's hands.
- Bring the right-hand corner over and tuck it under their back on the left side.

Safety tips

- Leave your baby to lie on their back when swaddled.
- Make sure the baby is not over-dressed (no more than a vest and babygro).
- Do not use extra covers unless the room is very cool.
- Make sure the sheet does not wrap around your baby's head.
- Avoid using a blanket with lacy holes in it.

Calming techniques

Self-calming

Young babies who are upset are less able to calm themselves without support and are unable to understand and manage the state they are in. They need help to actually deal with their distress, so that they are able to return to a more balanced 'happy' place.

However, babies are actually capable of calming themselves with the support of a loving, patient parent. By watching your baby, you will learn ways to support them when they try to 'self-calm'. For example, from a very young age, a lot of babies suck on their fingers or thumbs, as they find this extremely comforting. Sometimes your baby may manage to get their fingers into their mouth all by themselves; however, particularly in the early days after birth, they may struggle to do this and will need your help to guide their fingers. A little guidance from you can make all the difference!

Thumb-sucking is not the only comforting technique for a baby; there are many others that you might find your baby responds to. For example, some babies find it easier to manage their behaviour and become calmer when:

- they are swaddled
- they have the opportunity to focus on a patterned surface
- they are held in the Kangaroo Containment Hold (see below), facing towards a blank wall
- they are held in the Lazy Lion Containment Hold (see overleaf), looking towards the floor.

You may find the following holds are useful for your baby, particularly if they are in need of soothing.

Containment holds

Activity

The Kangaroo Containment Holds

- Whilst you are in a standing position, support your baby by cuddling them close to your chest with one arm and taking their weight with the other hand.
- Have their back to your chest, so that they are facing outwards.

Figure 6.2 Kangaroo Containment Hold (1)

Figure 6.3 Kangaroo Containment Hold (2)

The Lazy Lion Containment Hold

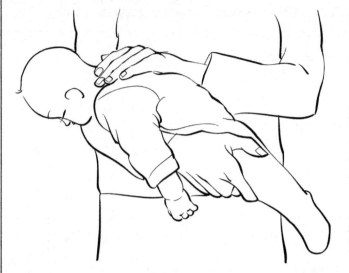

Figure 6.4 Lazy Lion Containment Hold

- Support your baby by laying them along one of your arms, facing downwards with their head by your elbow.
- Your arm should support their weight, whilst your hand is holding the top of a leg firmly.
- Rest your free hand on their back for extra support.

An introduction to massage for your newborn baby

The full massage routine may be over-stimulating for your newborn baby, so we suggest that you initially introduce your baby to some gentle stroking. Long, sweeping strokes over their clothes are particularly good for helping accustom your baby to massage. Your baby may find these strokes soothing and calming; although it is still important to watch for any negative cues (as described in Chapter 3). The full routine can be introduced gradually as your baby becomes ready for a more stimulating massage.

Activity

A suitable routine for your newborn baby

The following strokes are ideal to use when your baby is clothed.

Stroke A: Soothing Stroke

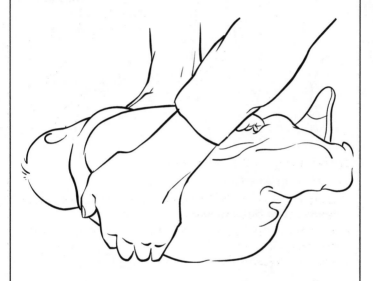

Figure 6.5 Baby on side

Either with your baby lying on their side (or in the Lazy Lion position):

- place a hand gently on your baby's head
- stroke down their back to their bottom
- repeat several times whilst talking or singing to them soothingly.

Stroke B: The Velvet Cloak

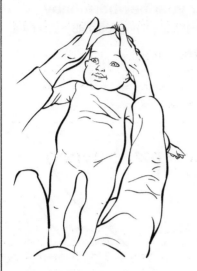

Either with your baby lying on their back on a changing mat or on your lap:

- bring both your hands to the top of their head
- using the flat of your whole hand, lightly stroke down the sides of their body to the feet
- repeat several times.

Figure 6.6 The Velvet Cloak

Stroke C: The Sole Stroke

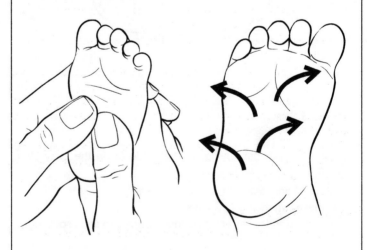

Figure 6.7 The Sole Stroke

Figure 6.8 Direction for the Sole Stroke

This stroke can be done immediately after a nappy change, before you re-dress your baby:

Either with your baby lying on their back on a changing mat or on your lap:

- with their leg slightly raised, cup their foot with both hands
- alternating your thumbs, stroke the sole of the foot, from heel to toes, fanning your thumbs from the centre to the side
- repeat three or four times on both feet.

Helping a baby feel secure during massage and yoga

Introducing massage

- If your baby is unhappy about being completely undressed, only uncover the actual area of their body that is to be massaged. Once your baby is comfortable with the massage routine they will be happy to be completely undressed.
- Some babies like to feel a boundary around them during massage. Create a boundary by:
  - rolling up a bath towel, length ways (like a sausage) and placing it around your baby
  - leaning against a wall, or solid piece of furniture, and cocooning your baby between your legs
  - using a changing mat that has inflatable sides. This may help your baby feel secure.
- Your baby may like to be massaged whilst they are in your arms. However, you will need to adapt the massage a little, so that you can manage with just one hand. This is a lovely way to do the massage, giving you the opportunity to have a cuddle at the same time.
- Chatting to your baby will help to reassure them during the massage, particularly if you speak in a soft, gentle voice or sing lullabies and nursery rhymes.

Introducing yoga

- The yoga moves are more energetic than the massage, so:
  - introduce the massage routine to your baby first
  - introduce yoga gradually, beginning with the Kangaroo and Lazy Lion Holds

  - start with the more gentle exercises that keep your baby close to you.
- Unless combined with the massage routine, there is no need to undress your baby.
- Just as you have done with the massage, use nursery rhymes and lullabies to reassure your baby.

Summary

- Swaddling may be useful to try with your baby, as they may enjoy the feeling of security and comfort this can give them.
- Understanding what your baby does to calm themselves when they are upset and helping them to achieve this when they are unhappy, will make them feel loved and secure.
- Containment holds, such as the Kangaroo and Lazy Lion Holds, may help your baby feel secure and will give you the opportunity to gradually introduce massage and yoga to them.
- Introduce massage and containment holds to your baby before the yoga exercises, so that they do not find it all too much.

07

the importance of music, singing and rhyme

In this chapter you will learn:
- why exposing your baby to music is good for them
- how babies respond to singing and nursery rhymes.

Sharing music with your baby

Once born, most babies love to listen to music. They will find certain types of rhythm soothing and comforting, particularly music that reminds them of the sound of a resting heartbeat. This is because, long before birth, babies continually feel the rhythm and hear the sounds from their mother's body, and a couple of months before birth they can also hear the sounds from the outside world, especially the tone of their mother's voice.

Without necessarily realising it, music can affect us in many ways. So often a piece of music or a particular song will conjure up an image, or remind us of a particular time or event that has happened in the past. With the image or memory, we often have a particular feeling come over us, which may make us feel excited or calm, happy or sometimes sad. Music can even affect our breathing and heart rate. The effect music can have on an individual is related to the key in which it is arranged. The keys F and C are considered to be particularly peaceful and can have a calming affect on babies, children and adults.

Activity

If you haven't already, why not try playing some soothing music to your baby and see how they respond. For instance, 'The Music for Dreaming' CD by *Sound Impressions* is so peaceful and calming and is a wonderful CD for both you and your baby to listen to.

Music is actually very similar to language, as they are both processed in the same areas of the brain and can contribute to overall brain development. For both music and language to be understood, they require an element of organization, structure, rhythm and a sense of timing; and both have various sound frequencies that make them interesting and gives them intonation and melody.

Using nursery rhymes with your baby during massage and yoga

It is the rhythmical aspect of both music and speech that babies may find soothing and comforting. This is why babies enjoy listening to rhymes that are sung, or spoken in a softer, slower and a higher than normal pitched voice. Some parents struggle with 'chatting' to their baby, but find that sometimes talking can be replaced with nursery rhymes that they feel more comfortable using. Babies seem ready to tune in to rhymes sung by their parents and tend to respond enthusiastically to this form of communication. They are able to follow simple rhythms long before they are able to speak.

The massage and yoga sessions will give you the perfect opportunity to introduce some rhymes to your baby. These will help to keep your baby focused on you, as well as giving you both time to share some special moments. You will probably find that your baby will begin to imitate the sounds they hear you make whilst you are singing. When babies do this, it is as if they are chatting or singing along, in their own way. When taking time to sing rhymes and songs to your baby, you will be giving them the opportunity to begin to learn about listening, joining in and the art of turn-taking during a conversation.

> **Good speakers and listeners are on the path to becoming great readers and writers.**

When you have the opportunity to recite rhymes, your baby will be listening to the sounds and the words. When singing to your baby is coupled with an interesting and enjoyable activity, such as massage or yoga, they are more likely to start to understand the meaning behind the words. For example, your baby will not understand the question 'Would you like a massage today?' However, when accompanied with the gentle stroking on the chest, they will, if massaged regularly, soon come to associate the words with the action and understand that massage is being offered.

> At only 4 months old, a baby is capable of responding to every type of sound produced by every language in the world. By 10 months old they are able to distinguish sounds from their own language (or languages) and are able to start making some sounds at this early age too.

Tuning in to variations in the voice

From about 2 months of age, a baby is able to process and respond to emotional and tonal variation within a person's voice. How rhymes are sung is important to how well a baby will respond to or appreciate them. For instance, a flat or monotone voice will not attract a baby to the singer, but a soft, higher than usual pitched voice will be more attractive for a baby and easier for them to respond to. The impact is greater if the important words or sounds are stressed and if the rhyme is repeated regularly.

As the voice goes up an octave or so, the developing brain responds by sending a greater number of chemical and electrical impulses along the newly developing neural pathways. This is an indicator as to how important singing to a baby really is. Which is further enhanced when coupled with play-time – which massage and yoga time can be considered to be.

Activity

To see how your baby responds to the variation in your voice, try saying the following nursery rhyme in a flat monotone voice. Then sing the same rhyme in a high pitched, rhythmical voice, stressing the word 'POP'.

Half a pound of tuppenny rice
Half a pound of treacle
Mix it up and make it nice
POP! goes the weasel.

As well as being quite a joyful, comforting and fun experience for you and your baby, repeating nursery rhymes so that your baby becomes familiar with them, can actually help with their cognitive development.

A baby to whom nursery rhymes are sung is more likely to develop a strong sense of well-being as they grow.

Listening to your baby

Massage and yoga will give you the opportunity to really watch and listen to your baby, giving you the chance to learn how they communicate with you. The sounds and little noises that babies make are more structured and controlled than is immediately obvious. But, if you take time to listen to your baby and enter into a 'conversation' with them, you will soon be able to recognize that your baby responds to your voice in a timed and specific manner.

> A baby that is listened to as well as sung to is more likely to feel calm, respected and loved.

Babies have a definite musical ability when communicating with their parents, the sounds they utter are in a timed, melodic sequence; and you might even notice that your baby will try to draw you into a 'conversation' themselves. If you do not respond to their first 'call' they will wait an exact, specific length of time, before each subsequent call trying to get your attention again. If you enter into a 'conversation' with your baby, you will notice that they pause for the same amount of time after each time you have spoken before they reply – as if they are politely waiting a few seconds, just to check that you have finished what you were saying!

Activity

When you have the opportunity to have a quiet moment with your baby and they are awake and alert, try having a 'conversation' with them. Simply say 'Hel – lo' in a quiet sing-song voice. Wait and listen for their response to your 'call'. Notice the length of time between your calls and their replies whilst you are chatting together.

Summary

Music:

- contributes to brain development
- improves verbal memory
- acts as a springboard for other skills to be developed
- is a powerful tool for supporting learning.

Singing:

- improves sound and rhythm recognition
- can help the development of speech and later, written language
- links sounds and visual images that are essential for reading and writing skills.

Rhyme:

- is something babies respond positively to
- means that babies soon become familiar with repeated verse.

08
the massage routine – getting started

In this chapter you will learn:
- how the learning programme is structured and the reasons behind the sequence of the strokes
- why it is important to ask permission from your baby
- the opening sequence to begin all massage sessions
- what to do after the massage and yoga session.

The massage routine

The following chapters (Chapters 9–13) give parents a step-by-step massage routine to follow with their baby once they are ready to experience the full massage.

Each chapter covers the strokes for one body area and allows you to learn and practise these strokes during the following week. If time permits, try to practise the massage strokes on a daily basis at a time that is suitable for both you and your baby. This will help you feel comfortable with the strokes and help your baby to become accustomed to the new strokes too. Each stroke has been given a suitable name to help you remember the full routine.

Try to follow the chapters for the massage routine in the order given. Starting with the legs allows your baby to become accustomed to the massage strokes, on what could be considered the least sensitive part of their body. The rest of the routine naturally follows up the front of the body and then on to the back.

Each week, start with the strokes for the new body area and then consolidate the body area(s) that have been learnt the previous week(s). This allows you to learn the new strokes first before moving on to and practising the previously learnt ones, should your baby be too tired to carry on. If you always started the massage with the legs, whilst working through the learning programme, then you might find it very difficult to progress to the new strokes if your baby becomes tired.

The learning programme

Week 1 – Legs

Week 2 – Stomach and Legs

Week 3 – Chest, Legs and Stomach

Week 4 – Back, Legs, Stomach and Chest

Week 5 – Head and Face, Legs, Stomach, Chest and Back

Week 6 – The Full Routine: Legs, Stomach, Chest, Head and Face, Back

---

The safest place for massaging a baby is on the floor with the baby on a soft blanket or changing mat, but parents must be mindful of their own comfort and think about position aids such as a cushion for the sit bones or leaning against a wall for back support, if needed.

Each chapter will contain:

- step-by-step instructions accompanied with line drawings to guide you through the routine
- hints and tips on safety during massage
- suggested nursery rhymes that enhance the enjoyment of each stroke
- alternative positions
- benefits for the baby.

The reasons behind the sequencing of strokes

Legs

To the untrained eye the leg sequence will appear to jump from one leg to the other and back again without good reason. However, there is indeed a very good reason for this. A baby's concentration span is very limited and although they may say 'Yes' to massage to begin with, within a few minutes of starting the massage this may change. If only one leg has received massage then the baby may feel slightly imbalanced as the massaged leg will feel relaxed whilst the other will still be carrying some tension. The sequence in Chapter 9 prevents this happening should the massage be cut short for whatever reason.

Back/head and face

Young babies often assume that 'food' is on offer when their face is touched due to the rooting reflex. As they develop and settle into a feeding pattern this becomes less frequent, so by leaving the head and face sequence until Week 5, this allows for the younger baby to progress to this stage.

Getting started

- Choose a time when your baby is happy to be massaged.
- Prepare the room: remember
  - subdued lighting
  - warm room
  - no overpowering fragrances
  - quiet space.

- Collect equipment, e.g. oil, wipes, towels, etc.
- Have this book to hand to learn the routine.
- CD player and relaxing music.
- Remove sharp jewellery and wash hands.
- Be mindful of your own comfort and use the alternative positions that are recommended.

Applying the oil

Patch-testing the oil

As a precaution, it is always preferable to do a patch-test first to check that the baby does not have an allergic reaction to the oil you have chosen.

- Rub a small amount of oil on the inside of your baby's wrist.
- Leave for 15 minutes.
- If there is no reaction, use this oil for the massage.
- If skin becomes inflamed and irritated, wash the area thoroughly with warm water and pat dry.
- DO NOT use an oil that causes a reaction.

Using oil during massage

- Warm the oil to room temperature for a short time before the massage session.
- There needs to be enough oil to lubricate the whole area to be massaged (usually about the size of a 10 pence piece).
- Put the oil in the palm of one hand.
- Rub your hands together to warm the oil.
- On the first application it may be necessary to apply a little more as some of the oil may be absorbed by your hands if you have particularly dry skin.
- Apply the warmed oil gently to the area to be massaged.

If, during the massage, there is a reaction from using any oil that you have already patch-tested, cease use immediately and wash the affected area with warm water. Pat the area dry and leave uncovered. Seek medical assistance if the irritation does not subside.

After selecting an alternative oil for future sessions, patch-test again but leave on for a longer period of time.

Gauging the correct pressure

There is no right or wrong pressure when massaging; every baby is different. Some babies quite like a vigorous massage whilst others would find this far too stimulating and would probably start to cry and show negative cues. However, even for babies that do not like a very firm touch, it is important that your touch is firm enough not to tickle them. Tickling can be far too stimulating and unpleasant for a young baby.

Whilst massaging your baby it is important, where you can, to keep at least one hand in constant contact with your baby's body. This makes sure that you do not startle them when you place your hand or hands on a part of their body that they are not expecting to be touched. Keeping one hand in contact with them will reassure them and make the massage far more relaxing.

> **Studies show that firm massage can be far more beneficial for babies than a lighter touch.**

After massage and yoga advice

After the massage has finished, it is advisable for parents to pay particular notice to the following:

- After the massage and yoga exercise your baby should be offered a drink as they may be thirsty.
- You should also drink after the yoga exercises.
- Wash or wipe your hands to remove all residual oil before attempting to move your baby.
- Wipe residual oil from your baby's skin, especially if bathing afterwards.
- Wrap or dress your baby after the massage to ensure they do not become cold.
- Often babies become sleepy after the massage, allow them to sleep or relax.
- Never allow a baby with oiled skin to be exposed to sunlight after a massage, as the oil may cause the skin to burn.

Asking permission

It is important to ask your baby if they would like a massage before you begin any massage or yoga. This will ensure that your baby feels heard and their feelings are respected.

Indeed, we acknowledge that this may seem rather a strange thing to do. You may feel that you are talking to yourself, knowing that your baby cannot understand you or reply back. However, week by week you will begin to recognize that your baby does understand and very soon you will be able to detect when the baby is saying 'yes' or 'no' to massage.

Before undressing your baby for massage, ask permission by:

- placing both hands gently on your baby's chest and rubbing gently in a circular motion
- looking into your baby's eyes
- asking your baby in a playful, melodious tone:

'Would you like a massage today (name)'

In the first week of practice your baby may not respond very clearly or even at all to this question as this is new to them too and obviously they do not understand what they are being asked. Because of this you may feel unsure whether to carry on with the massage or not at first, but very soon your baby will let you know, in no uncertain terms, whether they are happy with the massage or not.

With regular massage your baby will come to recognize that this question is the signal for massage and then respond accordingly. If they want a massage they usually become very excited and display many of the positive cues mentioned in Chapter 3.

Case study

'The first time I 'asked permission' from my 4 month old baby I felt very odd indeed. All the other mums in the massage group felt awkward too at first and we all let out an embarrassed laugh when our massage teacher asked us to do this. We overcame our unease and then got on with it. It didn't take long to get into the swing of asking Hannah for her permission to massage her. It made me realise that I was doing lots of things 'to' her but massage was a joint thing. It only took Hannah a few weeks to understand and when I asked if she would like a massage she would become so excited, kicking her legs and waving her arms and smiling at me and I was left in no doubt that she wanted to be massaged.'

The opening and closing sequence

Once your baby has given their consent for massage, the next step is to perform the wonderful opening stroke of the Velvet Cloak. This stroke is done when your baby is still clothed and signals to them that the massage is soon to begin. It also prepares their whole body for the massage. Once you have done this you can then undress your baby ready for the massage.

At the end of the massage session, no matter how much you manage to do, it is always good practice to finish with a Velvet Cloak too. This stroke is perfect for signalling the start and end of a massage session.

Asking permission

Figure 8.1 Asking permission

Figure 8.2 Direction for asking permission

- **Ask permission before undressing your baby.**
- Place your hands lightly on your baby's chest, rub gently in a circular motion and ask permission from your baby to massage them.

The Velvet Cloak (to begin and end all massage sessions)

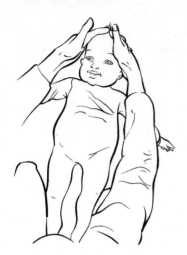

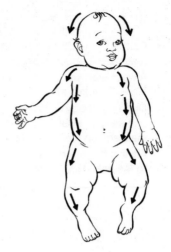

Figure 8.3 The Velvet Cloak

Figure 8.4 Direction for the Velvet Cloak

- Bring both hands to the top of your baby's head.
- Using the flat of your whole hand, lightly stroke down the sides of the body to the feet.
- Repeat three times.

Benefits:

- This stroke provides a gentle introduction to signal to the baby that massage is about to start or is coming to an end.
- This stroke prepares the whole body for positive touch.

Summary

- Always do a patch-test when using new oil to check your baby does not have a reaction to it.
- Always begin the massage session by asking permission.
- Do the Velvet Cloak over the clothes to let your baby know the massage is about to begin.
- Always start with the new strokes and consolidate the previous weeks' strokes afterwards.
- Once your baby is undressed, it is important to remember to try and keep at least one hand in touch with your baby during the massage so that they feel secure.
- Always finish a massage session with a Velvet Cloak to signal to the baby that the massage is coming to an end.

09

the massage routine – the legs and feet

In this chapter you will learn:
• the Programme for Week 1.

Upward Leg Stretch

Position
- Baby is lying on their back for all leg and foot strokes.

Tips
- Ask permission.
- Velvet Cloak.
- Remove clothes.
- Apply oil to both legs and feet (about the size of a 10 pence piece in the palm).
- Take care to glide very gently on the downward stroke. This prevents any undue pressure on the delicate valves in the baby's veins.

Suggested nursery rhyme:

Jack and Jill
Went up the hill
To fetch a pail of water

Jack fell down
And broke his crown
And Jill came tumbling after!

Benefits
- Promotes body awareness.
- Soothes sensory nerve endings, helping your baby to relax.

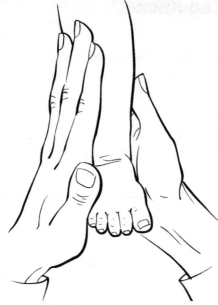

Figure 9.1 Upward Leg Stretch

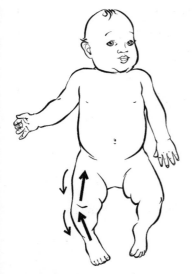

- Slightly raise your baby's leg
  by supporting one ankle with
  your hand.
- Using the palm of your hand,
  stroke up the leg from the
  ankle to the top of the thigh
  firmly and glide down the
  back of the leg from the
  buttocks to the ankle, gently.
- Swap hands and stroke up
  the leg again.
- Repeat three times with both
  hands.

Figure 9.2 Direction for Upward
Leg Stretch

Gentle Leg Knead

Tips

- Stay with the same leg, as with the Upward Leg Stretch.
- Take care to glide very gently over the knee.
- Take care to glide very gently on the downward stroke.

Suggested nursery rhyme:

Knead the dough
Knead the dough
When that side's done
It's over we go!

Knead the dough
Knead the dough
Bake it well
And watch it grow

Adapted from Knead the Dough *by Lowell Herbert*

Benefits

- Increases oxygen and nutrients to the cells.
- Encourages efficient circulation and lymph drainage.

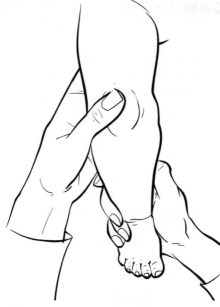

Figure 9.3 Gentle Leg Knead hand position

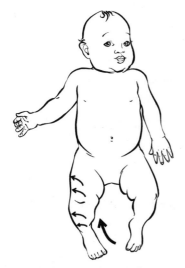

Figure 9.4 Direction of the Gentle
Leg Knead

- Slightly raise your baby's leg by supporting their ankle.
- Starting at the ankle – using the whole of your hand (thumb on top of the leg, fingers at the back) – knead one side of the leg towards the knee.
- **Gently glide the thumb over the knee.**
- Continue to knead from just above the knee to the hip.
- Gently glide your hand down the back of the leg to the ankle to maintain contact.
- Swap hands and knead the other side of the leg.
- Repeat three times.

Repeat the Upward Leg Stretch and the Gentle Leg Knead on the other leg before moving on to the feet.

Sole Stroke

Tips

- Stay with this leg.
- Take care not to tickle.
- For babies that have had invasive medical interventions, such as an intravenous cannula, take care if the area on the foot is still sore and be mindful that your baby maybe 'touch defensive' in this area.
- Take care not to twist the toes when rolling them.

Suggested nursery rhyme:

Windscreen wipers
What do you do all day?
Swish, swosh
Swish, swosh
I wipe the rain away

Windscreen wipers
What do you do all day?
Swish, swosh
Swish, swosh
I wipe the rain away

Benefits

- Increases circulation to the feet.
- Opens up the energy channels in reflexology zones.

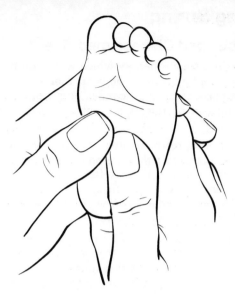

Figure 9.5 Sole Stroke hand position

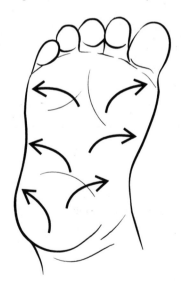

- With the leg slightly raised cup your baby's foot with both hands.
- Alternating your thumbs, stroke the sole of the foot, from heel to toes, fanning the thumbs from the centre to the side.
- Repeat three times.

Figure 9.6 Direction for the Sole Stroke

Bubbling Spring

Reflexology and Chinese medicine

Reflexology is a touch-therapy which works on the principle that all organs and parts of the body are represented on the feet. By applying massage to specific reflex points on the foot, areas of congestion can be released; helping with pain relief and relaxation.

Reflex points for the teeth are situated on the top of the toes. For the sinuses, eyes and ears they are on the underside of the toes. By massaging each toe these reflex points are stimulated, increasing energy flow to specific areas, which may help with teething pain, nasal and ear congestion. Reflex points for the brain are also found on the big toe.

Chinese medicine also works with pressure points in the foot. The Bubbling Spring stroke corresponds to the 'solar plexus' in the abdominal area. It is said that humans hold 'stress' in this area and by massaging this point on the foot, tension can be released.

Benefits

- Releases tension in the diaphragm muscle promoting deeper breathing and relaxation.

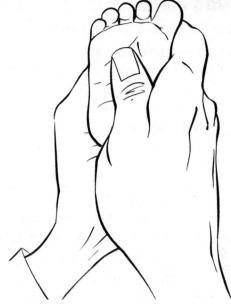

Figure 9.7 Bubbling Spring hand position

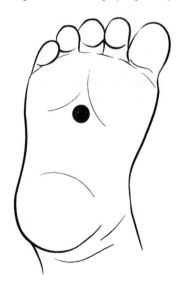

- Still keeping the leg slightly raised cup your baby's foot with one hand.
- With the other hand gently press with the thumb on the 'solar plexus' point firmly for 6–10 seconds.

Figure 9.8 Position of the Bubbling Spring

Toe Rolling

Tips

- Do not twist the toe when rolling.
- Take care to pull the toe very gently.

Suggested nursery rhyme:

Starting with the big toe:

This little piggy went to market
This little piggy stayed at home
This little piggy had a massage
And this little piggy didn't want one
And this little piggy said
'Oh, oh, oh I want one too!'

Benefits

- An opportunity for baby to visually observe their own feet, fostering body awareness.
- An ideal time to introduce language and counting games.
- Works on the reflexology areas that correspond to the head, sinuses and teeth.

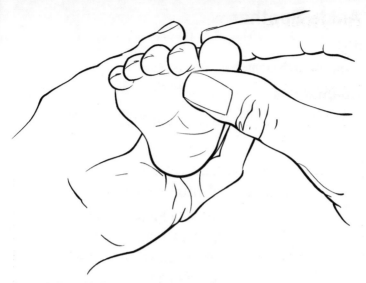

Figure 9.9 Toe Rolling

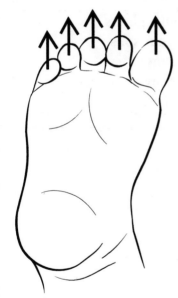

- Still keeping the leg slightly raised, cup your baby's foot with one hand.
- With the other hand gently roll each toe between finger and thumb from the base of the toe to the tip, starting with the big toe.
- Gently pull each toe at the end of the roll.

Now repeat all of these strokes on the other foot.

Figure 9.10 Direction for Toe Rolling

Ankle Soother

Tip

• Stay with the same leg.

Adaptations

• If your baby's ankle is particularly small use Position 2 (see opposite).

Suggested nursery rhyme:

Hot cross buns
Hot cross buns
One a penny
Two a penny
Hot cross buns

If you have no daughters
Give them to your sons
One a penny
Two a penny
Hot cross buns

Benefits

• Improves circulation to the joint, assisting general strength and elasticity of muscle fibres and tendons.

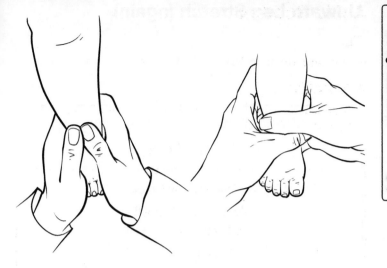

Figure 9.11 Ankle Soother – hand position 1

Figure 9.12 Ankle Soother – hand position 2

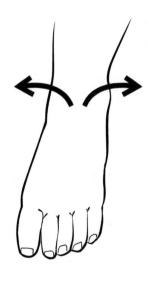

Figure 9.13 Direction for the Ankle Soother

- Still with the leg slightly raised, cup the heel with both hands.
- Stroke the top of the ankle, using your thumbs, from the front of the ankle to the sides.
- Repeat three times.

Upward Leg Stretch (again)

Tip

• Take care to glide very gently on the downward stroke.

Suggested nursery rhyme:

Horsey, horsey
Don't you stop
Just let your feet
Go clipperty clop
Your tail goes swish
And the wheels go round
Giddy up
We're homeward bound!

Benefits

• Promotes body awareness.
• Soothes sensory nerve endings helping baby to relax.

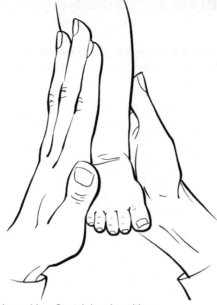

Figure 9.14 Upward Leg Stretch hand position

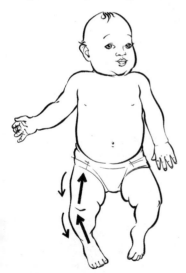

- With the leg still raised, support the same ankle with one hand.
- Using the palm of your hand, stroke up the leg from the ankle to the top of the thigh firmly and glide down the back of the leg from the buttocks to the ankle, gently.
- Swap hands and stroke up the leg again.
- Repeat three times with both hands.

Repeat the Ankle Soother and Upward Leg Stretch on the other leg.

Figure 9.15 Direction for Upward Leg Stretch

Jelly Roll

Tips

- It is important not to roll your baby's knee.
- Babies really love this stroke, so sing with gusto!

Suggested nursery rhyme:

Jelly on a plate
Jelly on a plate
Wibble, wobble,
Wibble wobble
Jelly on a plate

Jelly on a plate
Jelly on a plate
Wibble, wobble,
Wibble wobble
Jelly on a plate

Benefits

- Improves suppleness and elasticity.
- Induces relaxation by literally 'rolling out' tension in the leg.
- This is a great opportunity for you to have fun with your baby.

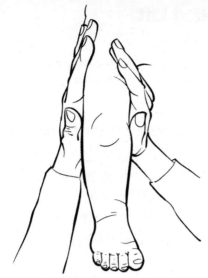

Figure 9.16 Jelly Roll hand position

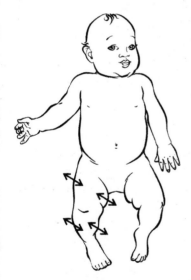

- Support one of your baby's legs upright by holding the thigh between both hands (as though making a dough sausage).
- Roll the thigh between both of your hands.
- Continue rolling up to the knee.
- Gently slide your hands over the knee to the calf.
- Continue rolling up to the ankle.
- Repeat three times.

Change leg and repeat.

Figure 9.17 Direction for the Jelly Roll

Double Leg Lift

Tip

• Take care to stroke gently down the back of the legs.

Suggested nursery rhyme:

Baa baa black sheep
Have you any wool?
Yes Sir, Yes Sir
Three bags full

One for the master
One for the dame
And one for the little boy
Who lives down the lane.

Benefits

• A good stroke to finish the leg and foot massage.
• Gently stretches muscles.
• Induces relaxation.

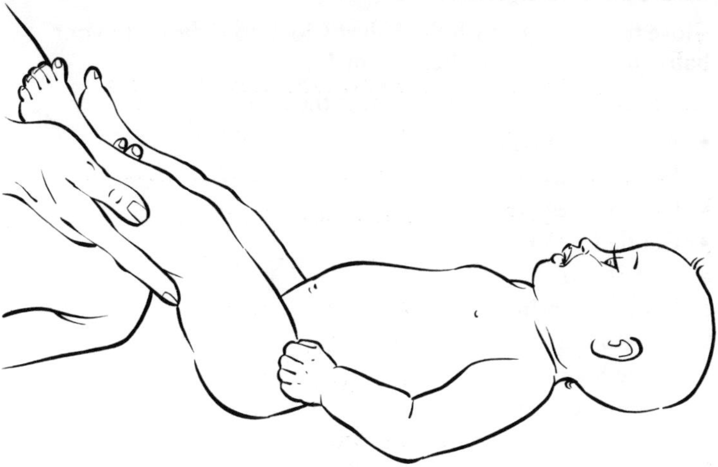

Figure 9.18 Double Leg Lift hand position

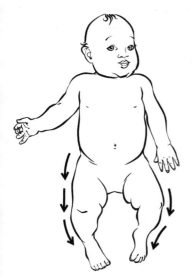

- Supporting the buttocks with both hands, gently stroke down the back of the legs to the ankles, giving a little lift and pull at the end.
- Gently lower your baby's legs to the ground.

Figure 9.19 Direction for the Double Leg Lift

Week 1 Summary

Close the massage with the Velvet Cloak to indicate to your baby that the massage has finished.

After Week 1 you will have learnt the following sequence:

• Asking permission
• Velvet Cloak
• Upward Leg Stretch
• Gentle Leg Knead
• Sole Stroke
• Bubbling Spring
• Toe Rolling
• Ankle Soother
• Upward Leg Stretch
• Jelly Roll
• Double Leg Lift
• Velvet Cloak.

10

the massage routine – the tummy

In this chapter you will learn:
• the Programme for week 2.

Tummy Hug

Position
- Baby is lying on their back for all of the tummy routine.

Tips
- Ask permission when in Week 2 of the learning programme.
- Do the Velvet Cloak when in Week 2 of the programme.
- Remove clothes.
- Apply oil to the tummy area.
- Remove the nappy for ease with strokes.
- **It is very important to remember – always stroke the tummy area in a clockwise direction.**
- **Do not press on the rib cage when performing the tummy strokes.**

Suggested nursery rhyme:

Pizza, pizza – it's a treat.
Pizza, pizza – fun to eat!
Stringy, gooey cheese so yummy;
Pepperoni in my tummy.
Pizza, pizza – it's a treat.
Pizza, pizza – fun to eat!

Benefits
- This is the 'opening' movement and indicates to your baby that the tummy massage is about to begin.

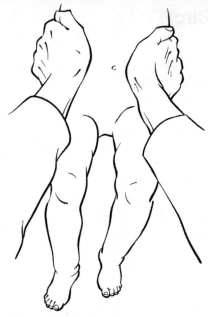

Figure 10.1 The Tummy Hug hand position

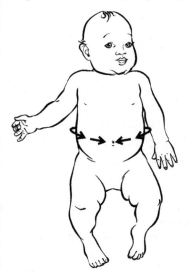

- Hold your baby by moulding your hands around their lower back and sides, your fingers not quite touching under your baby's body.
- Return both your hands from the back to the middle of the tummy area.
- Stroke just below the rib cage.
- Repeat three times.

Figure 10.2 Direction for the Tummy Hug

Tummy Circle

Tips

- It is very important to remember – always stroke the tummy area in a **clockwise** direction.
- Do not press on the rib cage when performing the tummy strokes.

Suggested nursery rhyme:

Round and round the garden
Like a teddy bear.
I'd better put my wellies on
Coz it's muddy out there!

Benefits

- A relaxing stroke that helps to warm the tissue in the tummy area.
- Gently increases the circulation to the tummy.

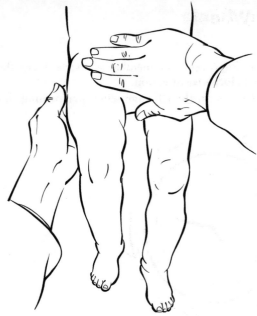

Figure 10.3 The Tummy Circle hand position

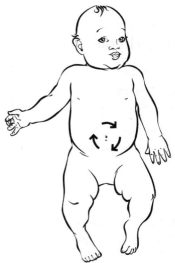

- Using the pads of your index and middle fingers, stroke a wide circle around the tummy button in a clockwise direction.
- Repeat three times.

Figure 10.4 Direction for the Tummy Circle

Daisy Wheel

Tips

- It is very important to remember – always stroke the tummy area in a **clockwise** direction.
- Do not press on the rib cage when performing the tummy strokes.

Suggested nursery rhyme:

Ring a ring o'roses
A pocketful of posies
ah-tishoo, ah-tishoo
We all fall down.

Benefits

- This is a slightly deeper stroke than the Tummy Circle and helps to move along trapped wind and helps alleviate constipation.

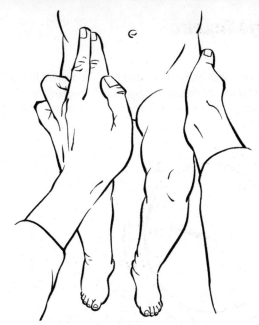

Figure 10.5 The Daisy Wheel hand position

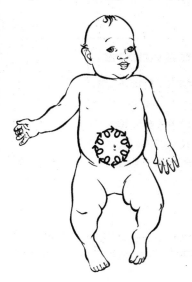

- Using the pads of your index and middle fingers, make small circles, like the petals of a flower, around the tummy button in a clockwise direction.
- Repeat three times.
- Finish with one or two Tummy Circles in order to be ready for the next stroke.

Figure 10.6 Direction for the Daisy Wheel

Tummy Square

Tips

- Always stroke the tummy area in a **clockwise** direction.
- Do not press on the rib cage when performing the tummy strokes.

Suggested nursery rhyme:

Doctor Foster went to Gloucester
In a shower of rain.
He stepped in a puddle
Right up to his middle,
And never went there again.

Benefits

- This is a slightly deeper stroke than the Tummy Circle and helps to move along trapped wind and helps alleviate constipation.

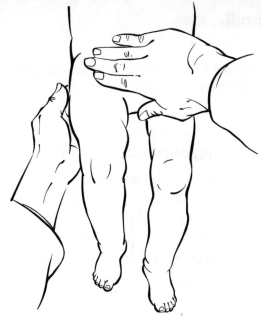

Figure 10.7 The Tummy Square hand position

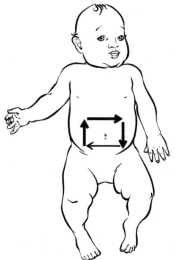

• Using the pads of your index and middle fingers continue the Tummy Circle once more.
• On the next time round add corners to the circle and follow the outline of a square around the tummy button in a clockwise direction.
• Repeat three times.

Figure 10.8 Direction for the Tummy Square

Windmill

Tip

- Take care not to press on the rib cage when performing the tummy strokes.

Suggested nursery rhyme:

Blow wind blow, and go mill go,
That the Miller may grind his corn.
That the Baker may take it,
And into bread make it,
And bring us a loaf in the morn.

Benefits

- This is a soothing stroke that will induce relaxation of the tummy area.
- Helps with bowel movements and alleviates trapped wind.

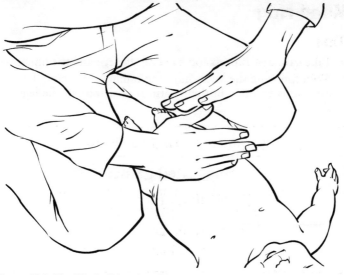

Figure 10.9 The Windmill hand position

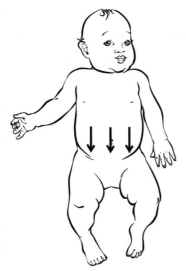

- Imagine your hands are like two paddles.
- Using the flat of both hands, stroke from beneath the rib cage to the top of the legs.
- Stroke down with one hand at a time like the paddles of a windmill.
- Repeat six times (three times for each hand).

Figure 10.10 Direction for the Windmill

Knee Hug

Tips

- Take care not to press too hard on the legs and the hip area.
- Avoid pressing the knees in to the tummy area, but allow the hip joints to open in their natural position (so the legs are slightly parted).

Suggested game:

Peekaboo! I see you!

Benefits

- This is a traditional yoga movement which helps release trapped wind.
- Relaxes tummy muscles.
- Gently stretches the muscles of the lower back and buttocks.
- Good opportunity for playful interaction with your baby when performed with the *Peekaboo* game.

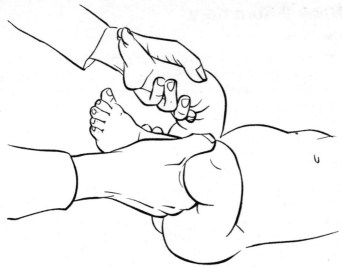

Figure 10.11 The Knee Hug

Figure 10.12 Direction for the Knee Hug

- Support your baby's ankles and lower legs in each of your hands.
- Bend their legs at the knee and very gently bring the thighs up towards the tummy.
- Hold for a count of six.
- Relax the legs down again.
- Repeat three times.

Week 2 Summary

After Week 2 you will have learnt and practised the following sequence:

- Asking permission – practise
- Velvet Cloak – practise

- Tummy Hug – new
- Tummy Circle – new
- Daisy Wheel – new
- Tummy Square – new
- Windmill – new
- Knee Hug – new

- Upward Leg Stretch – practise
- Gentle Leg Knead – practise
- Sole Stroke – practise
- Bubbling Spring – practise
- Toe Rolling – practise
- Ankle Soother – practise
- Upward Leg Stretch – practise
- Jelly Roll – practise
- Double Leg Lift – practise
- Velvet Cloak – practise.

Colic routine

To help babies suffering from colic, try the following routine approximately one hour before the onset of the colic. See Chapter 2 for more information.

- Windmill – Repeat six times.
- Tummy Circle – Repeat three times.
- Knee Hug – Once.

Repeat this sequence three times.

11

the massage routine – the chest, arms and hands

Loving Heart

Position

- Lay your baby on their back for all chest and arm strokes.

Tips

- Remember to ask permission when in Week 3 of the learning programme.
- Remember to do the Velvet Cloak when in Week 3 of the programme.
- Remove your baby's clothes.
- Apply oil to the chest area.
- Refrain from bringing your hands down to your baby's tummy during these strokes.
- You can leave your baby's nappy on just for the chest strokes.
- Some babies are not comfortable with their chest, arms or hands being massaged, be guided by your baby's cues.

Suggested nursery rhyme:

Hickory Dickory Dock,
The mouse ran up the clock;
The clock struck one
And down he did run,
Hickory Dickory Dock.

Benefits

- This is the 'opening' stroke and helps relax and tone chest muscles.
- Improves circulation, lymph drainage and breathing capacity.

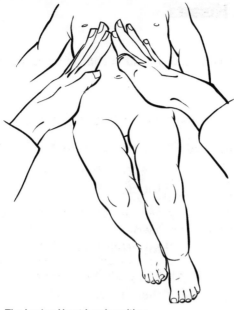

Figure 11.1 The Loving Heart hand position

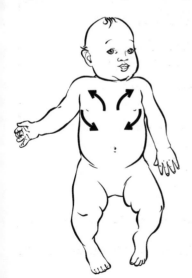

- Lay both hands on your baby's chest.
- Slide your hands up the middle of their chest towards the shoulders.
- Cup the shoulders gently.
- In a gentle sweeping movement, follow down the sides of the chest.
- Repeat three times.

This stroke resembles a heart-shape.

Figure 11.2 Direction for the Loving Heart

Loving Kisses

Tip

- Take care to keep one hand in contact with your baby at all times.

Suggested nursery rhyme:

Hot cross buns
Hot cross buns
One a penny
Two a penny
Hot cross buns

If you have no daughters
Give them to your sons
One a penny
Two a penny
Hot cross buns

Benefits

- Improves circulation, lymph drainage and breathing capacity.
- Improves body awareness and coordination by crossing the mid-line of the body.

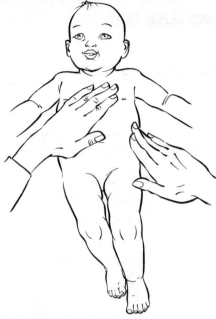

Figure 11.3 Loving Kisses hand position

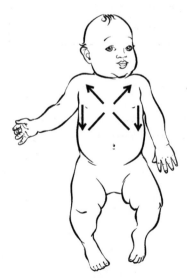

- Place both your hands either side of your baby's ribcage, near their waist.
- Using one hand at a time slide your hand up to the opposite shoulder.
- Cup the shoulder.
- Slide your hands down the side of the rib cage.
- Using the other hand, repeat on the opposite side of the chest.
- Repeat each hand three times.

Figure 11.4 Direction for Loving Kisses

Chest And Arm Glide

Tip

- Take care not to start below the ribs as this may cause some discomfort when gliding up the chest.

Suggested nursery rhyme:

Baa baa black sheep
Have you any wool?
Yes Sir, Yes Sir
Three bags full

One for the master
One for the dame
And one for the little boy
Who lives down the lane

Benefits

- Emphasizes body awareness and wholeness.

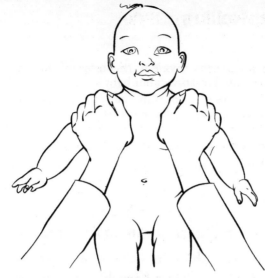

Figure 11.5 The Chest and Arm Glide hand position

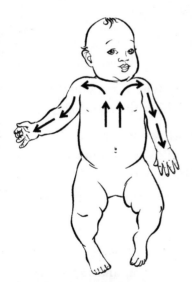

- Place both your hands flat on your baby's chest.
- Slide your hands up the chest.
- Cup the shoulders.
- Gently stroke down the arms to the wrists.
- Finish by opening your baby's palms gently with your thumbs.
- Repeat three times.

Figure 11.6 Direction for the Chest and Arm Glide

Finger Rolling

Tips

- When singing the rhyme to this movement, at the prompt 'how do you do?' shake your baby's hand very gently.
- Smaller babies may not want the hand strokes, keep trying to introduce them at regular intervals.

Adaptation

- Your baby may be seated for the hand massage strokes.

Suggested nursery rhyme:

Tommy Thumb, Tommy Thumb, where are you?
Here I am, Here I am, how do you do?

Peter Pointer, Peter Pointer, where are you?
Here I am, Here I am, how do you do?

Toby Tall, Toby Tall, where are you?
Here I am, Here I am, how do you do?

Ruby Ring, Ruby Ring, where are you?
Here I am, Here I am, how do you do?

Baby Small, Baby Small, where are you?
Here I am, Here I am, how do you do?
(Last verse said quietly.)

Benefits

- Provides opportunity to talk and sing and can be done anywhere at anytime.
- The hands mirror the reflexology points of the toes so Finger Rolling can help with teething and snuffles.
- Good for opening up and relaxing clenched fists.

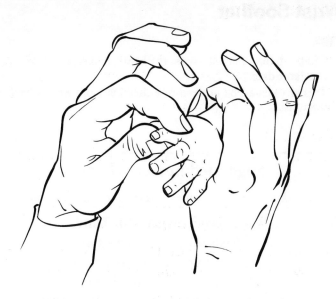

Figure 11.7 Finger Rolling

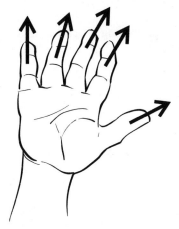

Figure 11.8 Direction for
Finger Rolling

- Support your baby's hand in one of your hands and perform the movement with your free hand.
- Start with the thumb.
- Roll each of your baby's fingers between your fore finger and thumb from the base of their finger to the tip.
- At the tip give a gentle squeeze and move onto the next finger.

Wrist Soother

Tips

- Smaller babies may not want the hand strokes, try them again at a later date.
- This stroke can be applied to either the front or the back of the wrist.

Suggested nursery rhyme:

Sing this verse to the tune of *Row, row, row your boat.*

Wash, wash, wash your hands,
Wash those germs away.
Soap and water does the trick,
To keep them clean all day.

Benefits

- Improves circulation to the joint, promoting general strength and elasticity of muscles and tendons.

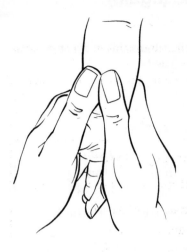

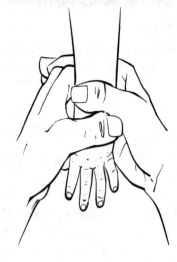

Figure 11.9 The Wrist Soother hand position (1)

Figure 11.10 The Wrist Soother hand position (2)

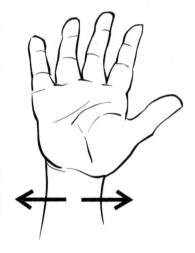

- Supporting your baby's hand, place both your thumbs on either the inside or the outside of their wrist and cup the back of the wrist with your fingers.
- Stroke the wrist from the centre to the sides using both thumbs.
- Repeat three times.

Repeat the Finger Rolling and the Wrist Soother on the other hand.

Figure 11.11 Direction for the Wrist Soother

Chest And Arm Glide (again)

Tip

- Take care not to start below the ribs as this may cause some discomfort when gliding up the chest.

Suggested nursery rhyme:

Sing a song of sixpence, a pocket full of rye;
Four and twenty blackbirds baked in a pie.
When the pie was opened, the birds began to sing;
Was not that a dainty dish to set before the King?

Benefits

- Emphasizes body awareness and wholeness.
- This stroke soothes and integrates the whole body.

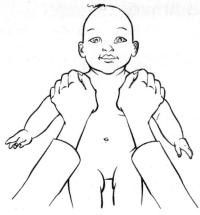

Figure 11.12 The Chest and Arm Glide hand position

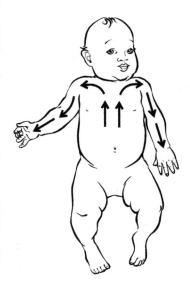

Figure 11.13 Direction for repeated Chest and Arm Glide

- Place both your hands flat on your baby's chest.
- Slide your hands up the chest.
- Cup the shoulders.
- Gently stroke down the arms to the wrists.
- Finish by opening the palms gently with your thumbs.
- Repeat three times.

Week 3 summary

After Week 3 you will have learnt and practised the following
sequence:

- Asking permission – practise
- Velvet Cloak to start – practise
- Loving Heart – new
- Loving Kisses – new
- Chest and Arm Glide – new
- Finger Rolling – new
- Wrist Soother – new
- Chest and Arm Glide – new

- Upward Leg Stretch – practise
- Gentle Leg Knead – practise
- Sole Stroke – practise
- Bubbling Spring – practise
- Toe Rolling – practise
- Ankle Soother – practise
- Upward Leg Stretch – practise
- Jelly Roll – practise
- Double Leg Lift – practise
- Tummy Hug – practise
- Tummy Circle – practise
- Daisy Wheel – practise
- Tummy Square – practise
- Windmill – practise
- Knee Hug – practise
- Velvet Cloak to close – practise.

12

the massage routine – the back

In this chapter you will learn:
- for Programme for week 4.

Position advice for back massage

It is useful to help your baby become accustomed to being on their front (See Chapter 2 for Prone Position) at least a couple of weeks before practising the back massage. Then your baby should be more comfortable in this position.

However, your baby may prefer to be in contact with you during their back massage so the following diagrams display three alternative positions for your baby during this massage.

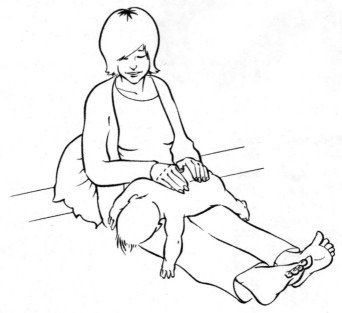

Figure 12.1 Position 1

- When your baby is lying across your lap, make sure that your thighs are pressed together. Any gap between the legs will cause your baby's back to hyper-extend. It may be more comfortable to have a rolled up towel between your legs to help support your baby's back.
- Place a towel across your lap.
- Ensure your baby's nose and mouth are clear of your thigh so they can breathe properly.
- Do not allow their head to hang unsupported.

- Have one of your legs stretched out and the other bent into the stretched leg, so that the sole of your foot rests on your inner thigh.
- Place a towel over your bent leg.
- Place your baby across the crook of the bent leg with their head towards the bent knee. This prevents the baby's back from hyper-extending.
- Ensure their nose and mouth are not obstructed.
- Place a small mirror on the floor beneath an older baby's head for extra fun!

Figure 12.2 Position 2

- If your baby prefers close contact, place a bean bag or large cushion against a wall and lean back.
- Lay your baby against your chest supporting their buttocks with one hand.
- Adapt the massage strokes slightly so they can be done with one hand.

> **CAUTION**
>
> **It is extremely important to work on either side of the spine, not on the spine itself, when massaging the back.**

Figure 12.3 Position 3

Back Velvet Cloak

Position
- Lay your baby on their front, in the Prone Position, with head to one side for all the back strokes.

Tips
- Remember to ask permission when in Week 4 of the learning programme.
- Remember to do the Velvet Cloak when in Week 4 of the programme.
- Remove your baby's clothes.
- This is a good stroke to oil the back completely before the back massage begins.
- **It is extremely important to work on either side of the spine, not on the spine itself, when massaging the back.**
- Use the alternative positions with baby on your lap if they want to be close.
- If your baby is on your lap, place a small mirror on the floor beneath them for added fun.

Suggested nursery rhyme:
Substitute baby's name in (name)

Rain, rain, go away,
Come again another day;
Little [*name*] wants to play.

Rain, rain, go away,
Come again another day.

Rain, rain, go to Spain.
Never show your face again.

Benefits
- This is the 'opening' stroke for the back massage and helps your baby to become familiar with touch to their back.

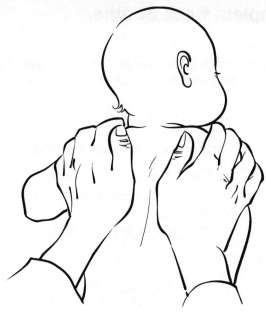

Figure 12.4 The Back Velvet Cloak (hand position)

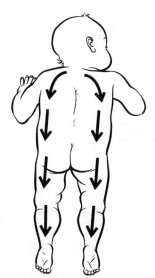

- Stroke from your baby's shoulders down to the ankles.
- Remember to lighten the stroke from the buttocks to the ankles.
- Repeat three times.

Figure 12.5 Direction for the Back Velvet Cloak

Complete Back Soother

Tip

- Take care to keep one hand in contact with your baby at all times, so your baby feels secure whilst they cannot see you.

Suggested nursery rhyme:

The little fuzzy caterpillar,
Curled up on a leaf,
Spun her little chrysalis,
And then fell fast asleep.

While she was sleeping,
She dreamed that she could fly,
And later when she woke up
She was a butterfly!

Benefits

- Soothing and relaxing.
- This stroke provides full body integration and feelings of wholeness and connection for the baby.

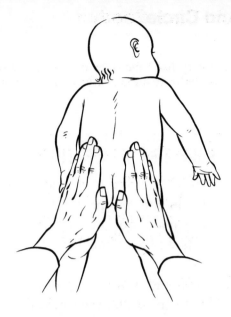

Figure 12.6 The Complete Back Soother

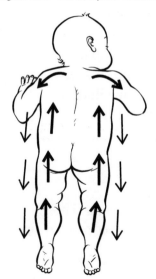

Figure 12.7 Direction for the Complete Back Soother

- Start at your baby's ankles, stroke up both legs and continue up their back (fingers either side of the spine).
- Lightly cup their shoulders and stroke down the arms.
- Slide hands back to the shoulders.
- Slide hands down to the ankles along the sides of the back and the legs (lighten the stroke from the buttocks to the ankles).
- Repeat three times.

Glide And Circle

Tip

- Take care not to hold the sides of your baby during this stroke, as this may tickle when your hands move up their back.

Suggested nursery rhyme:

Go in and out the window,
Go in and out the window,
Go in and out the window,
As we have done before.

Go up and down the staircase,
Go up and down the staircase,
Go up and down the staircase,
As we have done before.

Go round and round the village,
Go round and round the village,
Go round and round the village,
As we have done before.

Benefits

- Increases circulation to the muscles along the spine.
- Assists the development of muscle tone and postural support.
- Induces feelings of relaxation.

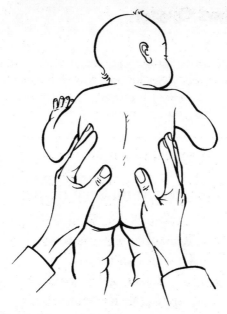

Figure 12.8 Glide And Circle hand position

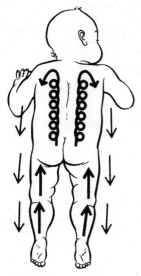

Figure 12.9 Direction for Glide And Circle

- Place both your hands flat on your baby's ankles and glide your hands up their legs over the buttocks.
- With the pads of the thumbs or the first two fingers, make tiny circles either side of the spine up to the shoulders.
- (Optional – before working on the back, circle the thumbs on the buttocks.)
- Glide hands back to the ankles (remember to lighten the stroke from the buttocks to the ankles).
- Repeat three times.

Glide And Stretch

Tips

- Take care not to hold the sides of your baby as this may tickle when your hands move up their back.
- Remember to lighten the stroke from the buttocks to the ankles so that you are working with the flow of blood in the veins.

Suggested nursery rhyme:

Wee Willie Winkie
Runs through the town,
Upstairs and downstairs
In his nightgown.
Rapping at the windows,
Crying through the lock,
'Are the children all in bed?
For it's now eight o'clock'.

Benefits

- Improves posture, muscle tone and general flexibility.

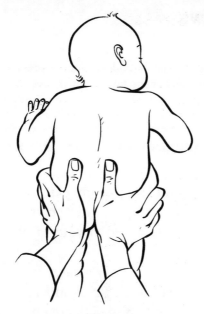

Figure 12.10 Glide And Stretch hand position

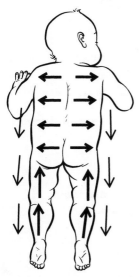

Figure 12.11 Direction for Glide And Stretch

- Place both your hands flat on the ankles and glide your hands up the legs and over your baby's buttocks.
- Place your thumbs either side of the spine.
- Stroke the thumbs out from the spine to the side of the body.
- Move your hands up slightly after each full stroke out to the side.
- Continue up to the shoulders.
- Glide hands back to the ankles (remember to lighten the stroke from the buttocks to the ankles).
- Repeat three times.

Cat's Paws

Tips

- Use one hand or two, but **do not** put any pressure on the spine.
- Only use the pads of the fingers for this stroke.

Suggested nursery rhyme:

I'm only a cat,
And I stay in my place...
Up there on your chair,
On your bed or your face!

I'm only a cat,
And I don't finick much...
I'm happy with cream
And anchovies and such!

I'm only a cat,
And we'll get along fine...
As long as you know
I'm not yours... you're all mine!

Benefits

- Deeply relaxing movement to close the massage.
- Soothes the sensory receptors in the skin.

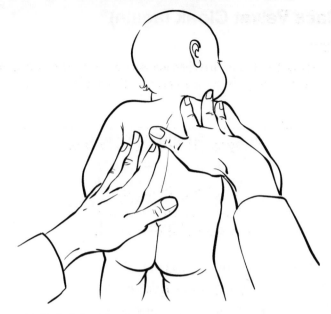

Figure 12.12 Cat's Paws hand position

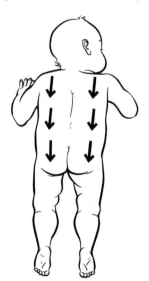

Figure 12.13 Direction for Cat's Paws

- Use your fingers opened out like a cat's paws (but without the claws!).
- Stroke from the shoulders down to the buttocks, either side of the spine, using one hand.
- Repeat with the other hand.
- Alternate hands three times.

Back Velvet Cloak (again)

Tip

• This stroke signals that the back massage is coming to a close.

Suggested nursery rhyme:

Half a pound of tuppenny rice,
Half a pound of treacle.
That's the way the money goes,
Pop! goes the weasel.

Up and down the City road,
In and out the Eagle,
That's the way the money goes,
Pop! goes the weasel.

Benefits

• Soothing and relaxing.

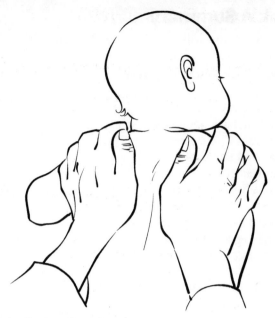

Figure 12.14 The Back Velvet Cloak

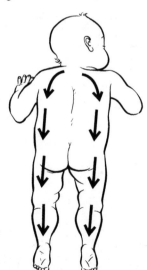

- Stroke from the shoulders down to the ankles.
- Remember to lighten the stroke from the buttocks to the ankles.
- Repeat three times.

Figure 12.15 Direction for the Back Velvet Cloak

Week 4 Summary

After Week 4 you will have learnt and practised the following sequence:

- Velvet Cloak to start – practise

- Back Velvet Cloak – new
- Complete Back Soother – new
- Glide And Circle – new
- Glide And Stretch – new
- Light Cat's Paws – new
- Back Velvet Cloak – new

- Upward Leg Stretch – practise
- Gentle Leg Knead – practise
- Sole Stroke – practise
- Bubbling Spring – practise
- Toe Rolling – practise
- Ankle Soother – practise
- Upward Leg Stretch – practise
- Jelly Roll – practise
- Double Leg Lift – practise
- Tummy Hug – practise
- Tummy Circle – practise
- Daisy Wheel – practise
- Tummy Square – practise
- Windmill – practise
- Knee Hug – practise
- Loving Heart – practise
- Loving Kisses – practise
- Chest And Arm Glide – practise
- Finger Rolling – practise
- Wrist Soother – practise
- Chest And Arm Glide – practise
- Velvet Cloak to close – practise.

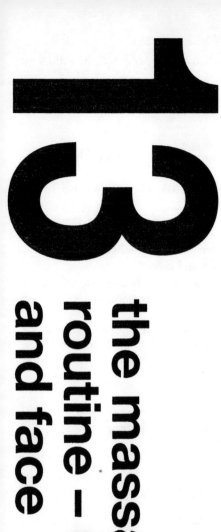

13

the massage routine – head and face

In this chapter you will learn:
• the Programme for week 5.

Angel Kisses

Position

- Your baby can be lying on their back or in a sitting position for the head strokes.

Tips

- Remember to ask permission when in Week 5 of the learning programme.
- Remember to do the Velvet Cloak when in Week 5 of the programme.
- Some babies, particularly the younger ones, may resist head and face massage. Introducing them at a later stage, when your baby is used to a regular massage, is always a possibility.
- **Do not apply oil to the head and face.**
- Try to avoid covering your baby's ears during this stroke.
- Take care not to press on the soft spots (fontanelles) on your baby's head.
- When the full massage routine has been learnt, we recommend that the head and face is done before the back massage, so that the baby's position is not being changed too often.

Suggested nursery rhyme:

Fuzzy Wuzzy was a bear
Fuzzy Wuzzy had no hair
So Fuzzy Wuzzy wasn't Fuzzy
Wuzzy?

Benefits

- Relaxing and calming.

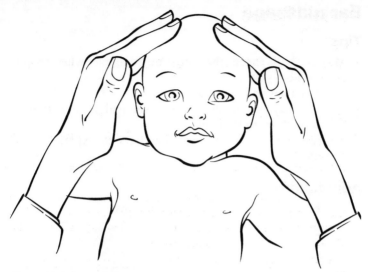

Figure 13.1 Angel Kisses hand position

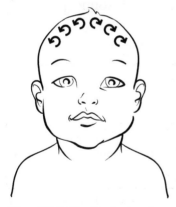

Figure 13.2 Direction for Angel Kisses

- Using both of your hands, make small circular movements with the pads of the finger tips – cover the whole of your baby's head, ending at their ears.

Ear massage

Tips

- Massage both ears at the same time (only one when baby is being held in your arms).
- Not all babies will like this stroke.
- The ears may become slightly red, even with little friction, as the blood flows to the helix.
- Practise this stroke on your own ears to experience the sensation.

Adaptations

- Can be done with your baby in your arms.

Suggested nursery rhyme:

Two little eyes to look around,
Two little ears to hear each sound,
One little nose to smell what's sweet,
One little mouth that likes to eat.

Benefits

- This massage will stimulate the auricular points within the ear (and has a similar effect to the reflexology points found on the feet).
- Helps to balance all of the body systems.
- Helps the blood circulation to the ears and helps the baby become more aware of their immediate environment.

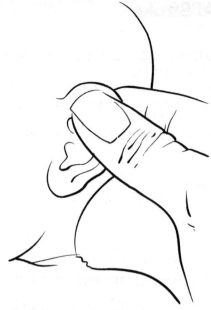

Figure 13.3 The Ear Massage hand position

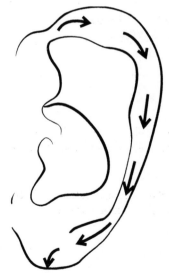

Figure 13.4 Direction for the Ear Massage

- Use your thumbs and forefingers and gently rub the rim of your baby's ears (helix) between them, starting at the top.
- Move down the ears slowly and continue down to the lobe.
- Now place the pads of your index fingers at the top of the rim of the ears again and in one gentle stroke follow the rim of the ears from the top, round and down to the lobe to soothe the nerve endings.

Forehead Stroke

Position

• Lay your baby down on their back for the face strokes.

Tip

• When holding your baby's head, take care not to cover their ears as this can be quite distressing for a young baby.

> ### Suggested nursery rhyme:
>
> Some little boys and girls I know
> Have freckles on their faces;
> Some, freckles on their nose and cheeks
> And lots of other places.
>
> I wish that I had freckles too,
> For everyone to see.
> I wonder what I have to do
> To have them land on me...

Benefits

• Can help loosen and drain mucus from the sinuses.

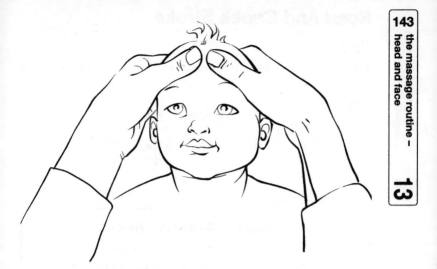

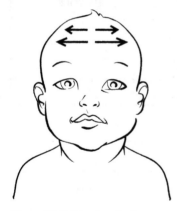

Figure 13.5 The Forehead Stroke hand position

Figure 13.6 Direction for the Forehead Stroke

- Place the flat of the fingers either side of your baby's head, taking care not to cover their ears.
- Place the flat of your thumbs on the middle of the forehead, above your baby's nose.
- Gently stroke your thumbs from the centre of the forehead to the temples, above the eyebrows.
- Repeat three to six times.

Nose And Cheek Stroke

Tips

- Take care with long nails when stroking down your baby's face.
- Do not cover the ears.
- Not all babies will be comfortable with this stroke, try again at a later stage.
- If your baby is suffering from a snuffle, use this stroke, along with the Toe Rolling, to help drain the sinuses.

Suggested nursery rhyme:

To be said/sung slowly and quietly.

There's a Big-Eyed Owl,
With a pointed nose,
Two pointed ears and claws for his toes.
He sits in the tree,
And he looks at you;
He flaps his wings,
And says Toowit-Toowoooo!

Benefits

- Can help loosen and drain mucus from the sinuses.

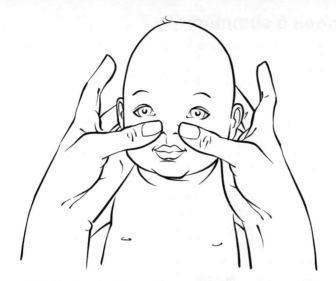

Figure 13.7 The Nose And Cheek Stroke hand position

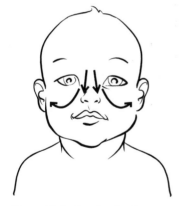

- Place the flat of your thumbs or the index fingers at the top of the nose.
- Using gentle pressure, stroke down the sides of the nose and along the bottom of the cheek bones, towards the ears.
- Repeat three times.

Figure 13.8 Direction for the Nose and Cheek Stroke

Week 5 summary

In Week 5 you will have learnt and practised the following sequence:

- Velvet Cloak to start – practise

- Angel Kisses – new
- Ear Massage – new
- Forehead Stroke – new
- Nose And Cheek Stroke – new

- Upward Leg Stretch – practise
- Gentle Leg Knead – practise
- Sole Stroke – practise
- Bubbling Spring – practise
- Toe Rolling – practise
- Ankle Soother – practise
- Upward Leg Stretch – practise
- Jelly Roll – practise
- Double Leg Lift – practise
- Tummy Hug – practise
- Tummy Circle – practise
- Daisy Wheel – practise
- Tummy Square – practise
- Windmill – practise
- Knee Hug – practise
- Loving Heart – practise
- Loving Kisses – practise
- Chest And Arm Glide – practise
- Finger Rolling – practise
- Wrist Soother – practise
- Chest And Arm Glide – practise
- Back Velvet Cloak – practise
- Complete Back-soother – practise
- Glide And Circle – practise
- Glide And Stretch – practise
- Cat's Paws – practise
- Back Velvet Cloak – practise.

The full routine

Once the five lessons have been learnt and practised you will be ready to carry out the full massage, in sequence.

The suggested routine is as follows:

Asking Permission

↓

The Velvet Cloak

↓

The Leg and Feet Strokes

↓

The Tummy Stokes

↓

The Chest, Arms and Hand Strokes

↓

The Head, Ear and Face Strokes

↓

The Back Strokes

↓

The Velvet Cloak

Enjoy the massage!

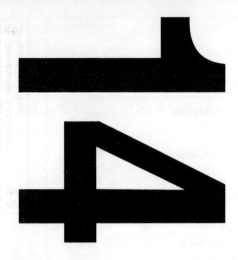

14

baby yoga – getting started

In this chapter you will learn:
- about some of the types of yoga
- how to manage the transition from massage to yoga
- what you need to prepare for the exercises.

Yoga routine

Chapters 15–18 contain clear and concise explanations and diagrams of how to carry out exercises based on yoga moves and stretches. As with the massage routine, there is a suitable nursery rhyme to sing with your baby that fits nicely with that particular exercise. For example 'The Grand Old Duke of York' is suggested for the Marching exercise.

Each chapter covers a particular area of the body and again, as with the massage routine, there are helpful hints on the safe way to practise the exercises and an explanation of the benefits. Where necessary, alternative positions are suggested.

Types of yoga

Yoga has been practised for thousands of years, but only recently adapted for babies so that they may gain from the many benefits associated with yoga postures (known as Asanas).

Yoga for babies can be active and dynamic and, paradoxically, relaxing and calming, so can offer stimulation for your baby when they wish to play vigorously; and then relaxation as they quieten and calm.

Type of Yoga	Characteristics	
HATHA (Gentle)	Focuses on holding poses.	Concentrates on slow stretches.
	Focuses on controlling breathing.	Builds flexibility.
		Focuses on deep breathing.
ASHTANGA (Active)	Focuses on moving quickly from one pose to another.	Very active. Improves concentration and stamina.
	Focuses on deep breathing.	Vigorous and fast-paced.
		Builds flexibility and strength.

Yoga is based on Asanas; breathing and, on occasion, meditation. Hatha yoga is commonly practised in the UK, although Ashtanga Yoga is gaining popularity. The majority of the exercises in this book are based on Hatha Yoga Asanas, but are fairly dynamic in order to maintain your baby's interest; although there is the opportunity to spend calm time with them as well.

Because baby yoga is more active than baby massage, it is important that you give consideration to your own posture, movements and handling of your baby. The yoga sessions give you the opportunity to think about relaxing by adjusting your posture and focusing on your breathing.

How to be focused on your breathing

Yogic philosophy believes that breathing strengthens overall well-being on a physical, emotional, mental and spiritual level. Therefore, correct breathing is of great importance, and 'pranayama' (yoga breathing) is considered to be as necessary for improving and maintaining good health as the yoga postures themselves.

> Pranayama is derived from two Sanskrit words:
>
> *Prana* (life force)
>
> *Ayama* (control)
>
> In its broadest sense, pranayama means the control of the flow of life force.

Consider how stress can make a person breath quickly and shallowly, yet by taking a deep breath they are able to quickly reduce the level of tension in their muscles, relax their posture and suddenly think more clearly and deal with the source of the stress – ultimately feeling more focused. So, breathing correctly may help relax and calm you and make you feel more grounded and clear-headed.

Benefits of pranayama

- Develops concentration and clarity of mind.
- Increases mental and physical powers of endurance.
- Induces relaxation, particularly for the nervous system.
- Increases oxygen supply to the brain.

Although the exercises in this book are for your baby, you may also benefit; particularly if you take time to focus on your breathing, if only for a few minutes, at the beginning and end of a yoga session (see relaxation techniques in Chapter 4). As your baby is attuned to how you are feeling, they will appreciate the calm time before and after the sessions, as much as you do.

Transition from baby massage to yoga

The following chapters give you a step-by-step guide to the yoga exercises to follow with your baby once you have learnt the full massage.

The chapters cover:

- legs, hip and tummy exercises (Chapter 15)
- arms, chest and back exercises (Chapter 16)
- baby/parent exercises (Chapter 17)
- yoga holds (Chapter 18).

If time permits, we suggest that you practise some or all of these exercises daily, so that you and your baby enjoy all the benefits of yoga. Each exercise has been given a name to help you remember them. In addition, the Asana name that the exercise has been based on has been included, along with its particular benefits.

You will see that the massage sequence is very structured; with a new sequence for a different part of your baby's body being covered each week. This helps to make learning the sequence easier; and helps with the flow needed to make the massage a pleasurable experience for you both. However, the yoga exercises do not need to be learnt and practised in such a structured way. It is a flexible routine that allows you to work with your baby and select the exercises that they particularly enjoy. In the early stages it is advisable to introduce one or two exercises from each section so as not to over stimulate your baby.

Each chapter will contain:

- hints and tips on safety during the yoga
- if relevant, the yoga name that the exercise is based on
- suitable nursery rhymes that enhance the enjoyment of the exercises
- step-by-step instructions accompanied with line drawings to guide you through the exercise
- benefits for your baby.

Gauging your baby's flexibility

The majority of babies are very flexible and can accommodate all of the yoga exercises. However, it is vital that you **do not** force your baby's limbs beyond their natural flexibility or beyond the point of resistance.

Getting started

- Choose a time when your baby is happy to do the yoga exercises.
- Prepare the room. Remember:
  - clear the space to enable you to move around
  - it needs to be as light and airy as possible.
- Collect equipment, e.g. yoga mat.
- Have this book to hand to practise the exercises.
- CD player and relaxing music.
- Remove sharp jewellery and wash hands.
- Be mindful of your own position when doing the exercises.

Asking permission

As with massage, it is important to ask for your baby's permission, before commencing the exercises, by:

- placing both of your hands gently on your baby's chest
- looking into your baby's eyes
- asking your baby in a playful, melodious tone:

  'Would you like to do some yoga today (name)?'

15

baby yoga – the legs, hips and tummy

In this chapter you will learn:
- legs, hips and tummy exercises, including:
  - Marching
  - The Jolly Jive
  - Budding Lotus
  - Tummy Turn
  - Leg Lift.

Marching

Position

- Lay your baby on their back for all the leg exercises.

Tips

- Use the Relaxation Technique (Chapter 4) to help you feel centred and calm before beginning the exercises.
- Remember to ask your baby's permission.
- Work with your baby's flexibility and muscle resistance, so as not to force their knees beyond the point of comfort.

Suggested nursery rhyme:

The Grand Old Duke of York
He had ten thousand men
He marched them up to the top of the hill
And he marched them down again

And when they were up
they were up
And when they were down
they were down
And when they were only half way up
They were neither up nor down!

Benefits

- Promotes body awareness.
- Soothes sensory nerve endings, helping your baby to relax.
- Helps release wind.

The yoga posture this exercise is based on:

Pavana-mukta-asana (The Wind Releasing Pose).

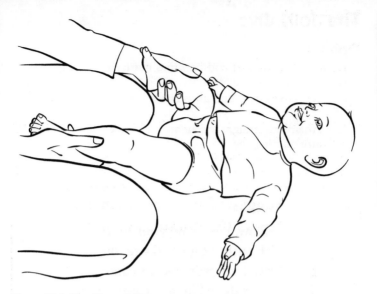

Figure 15.1 Marching position

- Support your baby's legs, by gently holding their ankles.
- Carefully bend each knee alternately up towards their chest (as if they were marching).
- Help your baby 'march' throughout the rhyme.

The Jolly Jive

Tips

- As your baby grows and becomes more robust, increase the speed, for a more fun exercise.
- Smaller babies may find all verses a little too much, so adapt accordingly.
- Keep their legs straight throughout all verses (without putting pressure on the knees).

Suggested nursery rhyme:

Row, row, row your boat
Gently down the stream
Merrily, merrily, merrily, merrily
Life is like a dream

Rock, rock, rock your boat
Gently to and fro
Merrily, merrily, merrily, merrily
Into the water we go!
'SPLASH'!

Swim, swim, swim about
Gently down the stream
If you see a crocodile
Don't forget to scream!
'Arhhhh'!

Benefits

- Strengthens and stretches the ankles and calves.
- Stretches the thighs.
- Maintains flexibility in the hip joints.
- Improves concentration.
- Improves sense of balance.

The yoga posture this exercise is based on:

Garudasana (the legs only).

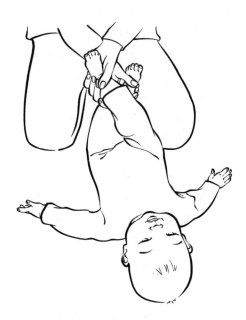

Figure 15.2 The Jolly Jive position

- Gently hold your baby's ankles.
- Continually cross and then uncross their legs.
- Each time you cross their legs, alternate which leg is on top.

Budding Lotus

Tips

- Work with your baby's flexibility, stop if there is any resistance.
- Rock gently in time with the rhyme.
- It is advisable to avoid this exercise if your baby shows any signs of hip displacement (normally identified during early health checks). If unsure, check with a medical practitioner before practising this exercise.

Adaptations

- If your baby is able to support their own head and back, this position can be done with them leaning against your tummy for support, whilst they sit between your legs.

Suggested nursery rhyme:

Rock a bye baby
On a tree top
When the wind blows
The cradle will rock
When the bough breaks
The cradle will fall
Down will come baby
Cradle and all.

Benefits

- Promotes flexibility and suppleness.
- Creates a natural balance throughout the body, mind and spirit.
- Enhances relaxation.

The yoga posture this exercise is based on:

Padma-asana (The Lotus Posture).

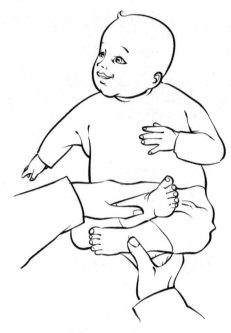

Figure 15.3 The Budding Lotus position

Imagine how a child would sit cross-legged on the floor:

- Bring your baby's legs into this position whilst they are lying on their back (or leaning on you).
- Gently holding their legs in this position, slowly rock your baby from side to side.
- Repeat with your baby's legs crossed over the other way.

Tummy Turn

Tips

- Work with your baby's flexibility and muscle resistance, so as not to force their knees beyond the point of comfort.
- Remember to circle their bent legs on the tummy in a clockwise direction.
- It is advisable to avoid this exercise if your baby shows any signs of hip displacement (normally identified during early health checks). If unsure, check with a medical practitioner before practising this exercise.

Suggested nursery rhyme:

Mary, Mary
Quite contrary
How does your garden grow?

With silver bells
And cockle shells
And pretty maids all in a row!

Benefits

- Helps release wind.
- Promotes suppleness.
- Maintains flexibility in the hip joints.

The yoga posture this exercise is based on:

Jathara Parivartanasana (Revolving Abdomen).

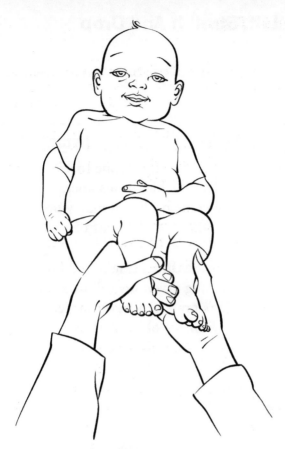

Figure 15.4 The Tummy Turn position

- Support both of your baby's ankles and the lower part of their legs with your hands.
- Gently bending their knees, bring their legs together so that their thighs are resting on their tummy.
- Support their legs in this bent knee position.
- Slowly circle their legs in a clockwise direction (so that the thighs are giving the tummy a gently massage).

Leg Lift, Stretch And Drop

Tip

• Take care not to stretch your baby's legs too vigorously.

> ### Suggested nursery rhyme:
>
> Bobby Shaftoe's gone to sea;
> Silver buckles at his knees.
> He'll come back and marry me.
> Bonny Bobby Shaftoe.
>
> Bobby Shaftoe's bright and fair;
> Combing down his yellow hair.
> He's my love forever more.
> Bonny Bobby Shaftoe.

Benefits

• A good exercise to end the leg sequence.
• Gently stretches the muscles in the legs.

The yoga posture this exercise is based on:

Supta Tadasana (lying down mountain).

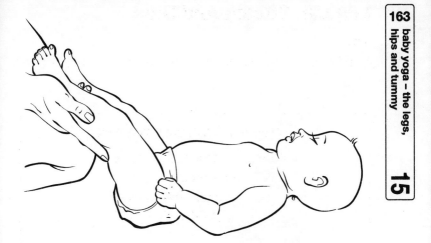

Figure 15.5 Leg Lift, Stretch And Drop Position

- Place your hands under both of your baby's buttocks.
- Gently stroke down the back of their legs to the ankles.
- Repeat three times, in time to the rhyme.
- Lift their legs slightly.
- Gently stretch the legs, whilst supporting their ankles.
- Take your hands away and let the legs drop to the mat.

16

baby yoga – the arms, chest and back

In this chapter you will learn:
- arm exercises, including:
  - Diagonal Boogie
  - Loving Hugs
  - Wind the Bobbin
  - Little Bird.

Diagonal Boogie

Position

- Lay your baby on their back for the arm, chest and back exercises.

Tips

- This exercise integrates the leg, hips and back exercises with the arms, chest and back exercises.
- Work with your baby's flexibility, do not force their limbs past the point of resistance.
- Do the exercise for one arm and leg during the first verse and then swap to the other arm and leg for the second verse.
- For young babies, the exercise and rhyme can be done at a slow pace.
- Older babies might prefer this exercise for longer and with more vigour.

> ### Suggested nursery rhyme:
>
> Cock a doodle doo
> My dame has lost her shoe
> My master's lost his fiddling stick
> And doesn't know what to do!
>
> Cock a doodle doo
> What is my dame to do?
> Till master finds his fiddling stick
> She'll dance without her shoe.

Benefits

- Promotes brain development (when crossing the mid-line of the body).
- Gently stretches the muscles in the arms and legs.
- Maintains flexibility in the hip and shoulder joints.

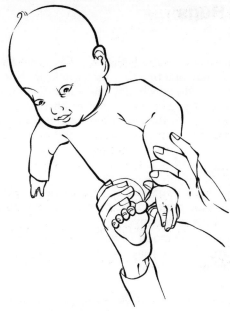

Figure 16.1 Diagonal Boogie Position

- Gently hold your baby's left ankle and their right wrist.
- Bring their leg and arm together.
- Then, stretch them out again.
- Repeat three times.
- Change over and hold your baby's other ankle and wrist.
- Repeat, as before, three times.

Loving Hugs

Tip

- For many of the exercises that involve both of your baby's hands, you may find that they prefer to keep their hands near or in their mouth, which may make it difficult for you to do the exercise. If your baby cannot be encouraged to join in, simply move on to the next exercise and come back to this another day.

Adaptations

- If your baby can support their own head and back, this exercise can be done whilst they are in a sitting position, supported by your tummy.
- Depending on the mood of your baby, this exercise can be done swiftly or slowly, as the selected rhyme lends itself to both a slow or a fast beat.

Suggested nursery rhyme:

Smiling girls, rosy boys
Come and buy my little toys
Monkeys made of gingerbread
And sugar horses painted red.

Benefits

- Promotes body awareness.
- Soothes sensory nerve endings, which will help your baby to relax.
- Stretches muscles between the shoulder blades.
- Expands the chest for improved breathing.

The yoga posture this exercise is based on:

Garudasana (the arms only).

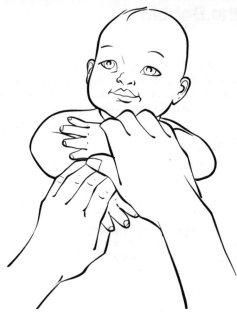

Figure 16.2 Loving Hugs Position

- Gently hold your baby's wrists and stretch their arms out to the sides.
- Bring their arms in towards their chest.
- Cross your baby's arms over each other (as if they were hugging themselves).
- Then gently stretch the arms out to the sides again.
- Repeat throughout the verse.

Wind the Bobbin

Tip

- As this exercise is quite stimulating, this may be a little too much for young babies. Introduce the first two verses initially, so your baby can become accustomed to the exercise and add the last verse when they are a little bigger.

Adaptations

- Your baby can be in a supported sitting position.

Suggested nursery rhyme:

Wind the bobbin up
Wind the bobbin up
Pull, pull, clap, clap, clap

Wind it back again
Wind it back again
Pull, pull, clap, clap, clap
And clap your hands

Point to the ceiling
Point to the floor
Point to the windows
Point to the door
Clap your hands together
One, two, three
Put your hands upon your knee.

Benefits

- Promotes body awareness and stimulates the senses.
- Stretching and relaxing.
- Promotes awareness of the surrounding environment.

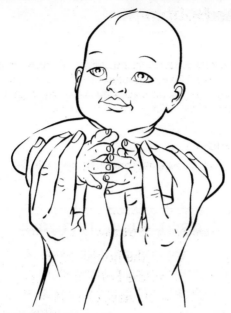

Figure 16.3 Wind The Bobbin position

- Gently hold your baby's wrists and bring them together across their chest.
- Circle their hands and lower arms around each other in a winding movement for the first verse.
- Stretch arms out to the sides then bring them in again to clap.
- Circle your baby's hands and lower arms in the opposite direction for the second verse.
- Stretch their arms out to the sides then bring them in again to clap.
- Whilst singing the final verse of the rhyme, follow the actions as described.

Little Bird

Tips

- Work with your baby's flexibility. Do not force their arms beyond the point of resistance.
- Try to keep their arms reasonably straight, like the wings of a bird.

Adaptations

- Your baby can be in a supported sitting position.

Suggested nursery rhyme:

See saw margery daw
Johnny has got a new master
He shall have but a penny a day
Because he can't work any faster.

Benefits

- Stretching and relaxing.
- Maintains flexibility in shoulder joints.
- Expands the chest for improved breathing.

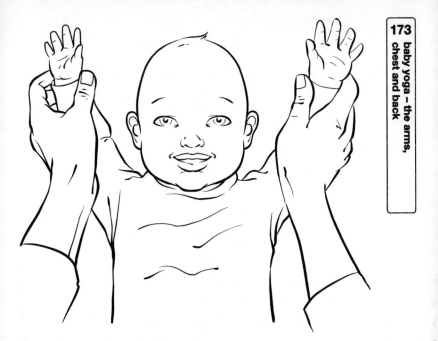

Figure 16.4 Little Bird position

- Gently hold your baby's wrists.
- Slowly and gently, stretch their arms above their head.
- Bring your baby's arms back down to their sides, as if they were a bird flapping their wings in slow motion.
- Repeat three times.

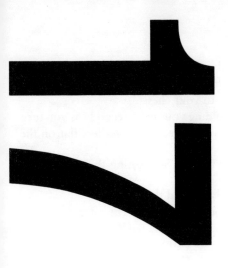

17

yoga exercises for your baby and you

In this chapter you will learn:
- exercises that benefit both you and your baby including:
  - Bell Horses
  - Roly Poly.

Bell Horses

Position

- After placing the your baby on a mat on the floor, you need to:
  - lay beside your baby, facing towards them
  - cradle your baby close to your chest
  - roll onto your back, holding your baby securely as you turn
  - lie on your back with your knees bent and feet flat on the floor
  - sit your baby on your tummy, supporting their back with your thighs
  - hold your baby securely around the middle
  - after the game bring your baby to your chest again and roll on to your side
  - lay your baby down before sitting up.

Tip

- This exercise requires reasonable abdominal and pelvic floor muscle tone, so stop immediately if it feels too uncomfortable.

Suggested nursery rhyme:

Bell horses, bell horses
What time of day?
One o'clock, two o'clock
Three and away!

Benefits for parents and baby

- Fun time for your baby whilst you exercise.
- This is based on a Pilates exercise that is excellent for helping tone the pelvic floor muscles, particularly after birth. It may help to strengthen your tummy muscles and tone your legs.

177
yoga exercises for your
baby and you

17

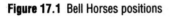

Figure 17.1 Bell Horses positions

- You need to slowly push your hips to the ceiling.
- Then lower them to the floor again.
- Repeat throughout the rhyme so that your baby looks like they are horse-riding.

Roly Poly

Position

- You need to:
  - sit on the floor with your legs stretched out in front of you
  - keep your legs together
  - lay your baby across your thighs.

Tips

- It is important to ensure that your baby's back is supported by keeping your legs together.
- For bigger babies roll a towel up and place it between your thighs.
- For smaller babies ensure their neck is supported.

Suggested nursery rhyme:

My bonnie lies over the ocean
My Bonnie lies over the sea
My Bonnie lies over the ocean
Oh bring back my bonnie to me.
Bring back, bring back
Bring back my Bonnie to me
Bring back, bring back
Bring back my Bonnie to me!

Benefits

- This may help to strengthen your baby's back muscles.
- Gently turning a baby helps develop their vestibular system.

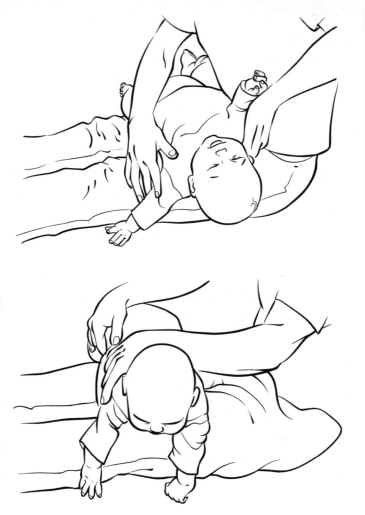

Figure 17.2 Roly Poly positions

- Gently rock your baby to and fro on your thighs.
- Continue rocking three times.
- Roll them all the way over, down your legs.
- Continue rocking three times.
- Roll them all the way over, up your legs, back to your thighs.

18

baby yoga holds

In this chapter you will learn:
- The Kangaroo Hop
- The Leaping Lion

The Kangaroo Hop

Position

- Whilst standing up, support your baby firmly by cuddling them close to your chest, with one arm.
- Take their weight with the other hand, by supporting them under their bottom.
- Have their back against your chest, so that they are facing outwards.

Tips

- When standing up from the floor, holding your baby, it is important for you to leave them on the mat until you are on your knees, in an upright position:
  - once on your knees, lift your baby from the floor
  - then, bringing one knee up so that your foot is flat on the floor, start to push up, holding your baby close to your chest. Take the weight on your bent leg and straighten up into a standing position.
- This is a secure hold that can be useful when the baby needs help to calm, if they are fractious.
- A good hold for both gentle and active standing exercises.
- As your baby becomes accustomed to this exercise, they may be happy for you to sing a nursery rhyme with more verses, so that the whole experience lasts longer.

Suggested nursery rhyme:

Jack, be nimble,
Jack, be quick,

Jack jump over the candlestick.

Benefits

- Allows your baby to experience different movements and see the world from different perspectives.
- Performing repetitive movements with a baby strengthens the neural pathways between their brain and their body.

Figure 18.1 The Kangaroo Hop Hold

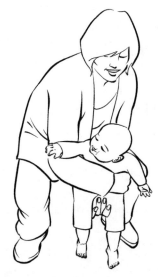

- Bend your knees and gently lower your baby towards the floor as if you were squatting.
- Then straighten your legs and lift your baby up towards your chest again.
- Repeat throughout the rhyme.

Figure 18.2 The Kangaroo Hop

Leaping Lion

Position

- Support your baby by laying them along an arm, facing downwards with their head by your elbow.
- One arm should support your baby's weight, whilst the hand is holding the top of one of their legs firmly.
- Rest your free hand on their back for extra support.

Tips

- This is a secure hold that can be useful when your baby needs help to calm, if they are fractious.
- Start rocking your baby to and fro gently, in time with the rhyme. As they become accustomed to this position and exercise, it may be more fun to swing a little more vigorously so rhymes with a faster beat may help.
- As your baby becomes used to this exercise, they may be happy for a longer nursery rhyme, so that it lasts longer.

> ### Suggested nursery rhyme:
>
> There was one little bird in a little tree,
> He was all alone, and he didn't want to be.
> So he flew far away, over the sea,
> And brought back a friend to live in the tree.

Benefits

- Encourages and supports the development of balance and coordination.

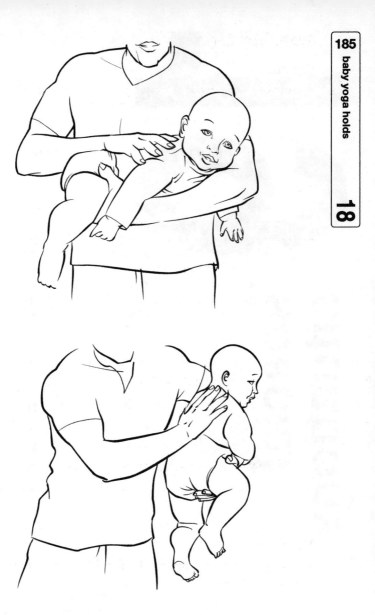

Figure 18.3 The Leaping Lion

- Throughout the rhyme slowly walk around, gently swinging your baby to and fro.

19
special
situations

In this chapter you will learn:
- how massage and yoga can help the following:
  - babies with special needs
  - special situations
  - childhood ailments.

Babies with special needs

Premature babies

Having to be on a neonatal unit can be quite stressful for a premature baby; partly because they have left the confines of the womb before they were at the correct stage of their development to do so; and partly because of the invasive medical treatment they receive in order for them to survive. Just being in the outside world can be incredibly stimulating for a premature baby and even the slightest touch can be all too much for them. In the early days after birth they will be far too sensitive to receive a full massage; and even light stroking may be extremely irritating and stressful for them. However, gentle positive touch may be comforting, without being over-stimulating and gives parents the opportunity to start to learn what their baby is 'telling' them.

Benefits for your premature baby

If the hospital neonatal staff encourage you to practise containment holds with your hypersensitive baby (Chapter 6) this can be extremely positive for you both. In fact, there is some evidence to show that some premature babies who get positive touch from their mum or dad in hospital can improve physically and mentally – they might even gain weight more rapidly.

Benefits for you, if you have a baby on the neonatal unit

If your baby is attached to wires and machines, you may be feeling helpless, powerless and detached from your baby. However, using positive touch with your baby can really help you too, because you are helping your baby, as well as having the opportunity to spend time getting to know them and start to build a bond with them at the same time.

> As your baby grows and develops, it will become possible to gradually introduce the gentle strokes and eventually most of the massage. But, it is not suitable to carry out yoga exercises with a premature baby, until they are fit and well and at least a couple of months past their original expected due date.

Tips for introducing touch

It may be necessary for you to introduce 'touch' to your baby in stages, so that you have the chance to really start to understand your baby's needs and not over-stimulate them with too much, too soon.

- *Skin to skin contact*, sometimes known as 'Kangaroo Care', is often a good first step to introducing positive touch to your premature baby. For this you need to tuck your baby inside your top so that your baby's skin is in contact with yours. This can be so comforting for them and gives you the opportunity to get really close.
- *Containing positive energy* – in some cases actually touching your baby may be far too stimulating for them. If this is so, simply hold your hands about 8–10 cm from your baby, so that they can feel your energy.

Activity

To see how your baby might feel your energy:

- sit quietly with your hands about 15–20 cm apart (imagine you are holding a ball delicately between your hands).
- concentrate on the area between your hands as you slowly bring them together.
- you should notice that there comes a point when you can feel the energy between your hands. It feels as if you have something there, but you can not see what it is. This is what your baby will be able to feel when you hold your hands about 8–10 cm above them.

- *Containment holds* to the head, chest, head and buttock, and head and back can be very beneficial, which may:
  - help to centre and calm both you and your baby
  - allow you to introduce some gentle touch to your baby
  - be comforting for your baby
  - help settle your baby when distressed.

Tips for introducing massage

- *Stroking* is often the first step to introducing massage to a premature baby. Once your baby is a little more robust and more accustomed to their environment, they may be ready to experience the benefits of receiving some massage – the long, slow, gentle strokes along the limbs described in the Newborn Routine (Chapter 6) are a good starting point.
- *Before massage* – Leave at least half an hour after feeding before carrying out any massage.
- *Once massage is introduced*, your baby may be more settled and enjoy the massage, if:

- the lighting is subdued
- there is gentle music playing in the background
- you only try a minimum number of strokes.
- **Being sensitive to invasive procedures.** Many premature babies experience invasive procedures during their time on the neonatal unit and many have cannulas in their feet. If this is the case with your baby, you may find that they do not like their feet being massaged. Simply hold their feet gently and talk reassuringly to them, until they feel more comfortable and begin to understand that the touch that you are offering is positive and loving.

Babies that have special needs

Coming to terms with the birth of a baby with special needs may be very challenging and difficult for many parents. The condition a baby is born with may affect not only the child's life forever, but it is likely to impact on the family as a whole. A baby with special needs may find it more difficult to respond to many of the usual signals that parents use to communicate with them (eye contact, smiling, speech and body movements) because of their particular condition. This may make the early bonding stage more challenging for parents. However, baby massage and yoga can help tremendously, because of the time it gives parents to really start to watch and then understand their baby. By their very nature, massage and yoga are very interactive, so they can help parents gain confidence when they are communicating with their baby. Through massage and yoga, parents can 'tune' into their baby and learn more about what their baby is trying to 'tell' them, even when a baby's cues are quite subtle. These activities also give parents special time with their baby, giving them the opportunity to really build their relationship.

As well as the emotional benefits to be gained from introducing massage and yoga to a baby with special needs, the physical benefits associated with these activities may also have a positive affect, offering parents a useful tool to enhance their child's potential physical ability and ultimately their enjoyment of life.

Pre-autism

Studies in many countries show that Autism appears to present itself in infancy as 'pre-autism'. This is whereby a baby will begin to show a number of recognisable characteristics. These signs of 'pre-autism' have been analysed with the use of video footage dating back to the 1930s.

It has also been recognized that the interaction and the subsequent attachment between parent and 'pre-autistic' baby was clearly different to that of a parent and infant, where the baby did not present with this condition.

A centre in Israel, studying pre-autism, offers support to parents with babies showing signs of pre-autism. They help the parents by teaching them how to improve the interaction and engagement with their babies. One of the tools that is used is baby massage – this helps with the interaction between parent and baby. The centre has been able to establish that intervention at an early stage definitely seemed, in most cases, to prevent the usual recognisable autistic characteristics developing later.

Autism

Children with autism are usually diagnosed at around 18 months of age. They often have difficulty in relating to other people, have a disassociation from their environment and are very sensitive to sound, light, smell and touch. Children with autism are often touch-defensive and can become aggressive when touched.

Massage may help a child by reducing their stress. It may also improve communication, such as eye contact and vocalisation. However, it is a light touch that can be far too over-stimulating for these children, so it is recommended that a firmer touch is applied. Always watch for their individual cues and be patient as they will not respond as quickly to massage as other children that do not have this condition.

Interactive play such as the yoga exercises and the massage stories can also help some autistic children. Shared play experiences can enhance a child's potential in all areas of learning and development. Interaction and communication with children using play rather than simply increasing 'play skills' can enhance their learning experience. For instance, introducing a basket of food for sensory input during the Pizza Massage (see Chapter 21) can really help with communication; parents can establish a connection with their child by exploring the sensory experiences they enjoy.

Babies with hypotonicity

Babies that are hypotonic have poor muscle tone and can appear floppy.

Tips for massage and yoga
- To help improve your baby's muscle tone:
  - the massage strokes you use should be brisk and stimulating
  - massaging the chin and cheeks can help support their tongue and help with speech.
- Be careful not to hyper-extend their, what appear to be, very flexible joints during the yoga exercises.

Babies with hypertonicity
Babies that are hypertonic have very tense muscle tone and can appear stiff and lack flexibility.

Tips for massage and yoga
- Initially concentrate on the unaffected areas of your baby's body so that your baby learns to appreciate how good massage and yoga can feel.
- Start with gentle massage on the affected areas of their body, as tense muscles can be tender when pressure is applied to them.
- To avoid discomfort, do not force your baby's tense muscles beyond their capacity during the yoga exercises. The yoga exercises for the affected area may not be appropriate, depending on the severity of the tension in their muscles.
- Continually reassure your baby during the massage routine and yoga exercises.
- Massage strokes and yoga exercises should be slow.

Children with visual or auditory impairment
Tactile experiences are of great importance for the visually and hearing impaired baby as they help them define the world. Massage can offer them a positive tactile experience.

Visual impairment: Tips for massage and yoga
- Talking gently and singing to your baby during the massage and yoga sessions is especially important.
- Describing the area of their body that is being massaged can promote body awareness.
- Holding and cuddling frequently gives reassurance and will help to make your baby feel secure.
- You can try and give your baby boundaries by putting a towel rolled up like a sausage around them, giving an added sense of security, during the massage and the yoga floor exercises.

- Reduce the noises in the immediate area to a minimum:
  - so that your baby is more likely to stay focused on you and will not be distracted
  - so that your baby feels secure.

Auditory impairment: tips for massage and yoga
- Lots of eye contact between you and your baby is important:
  - until your baby is used to massage and yoga and feels secure, avoid strokes and exercises that impede this eye contact (such as the back massage).
- Talking and singing rhymes to your baby is still important:
  - Your baby is more likely to focus on your lips as they move and may feel the vibrations from the singing.
  - This helps you focus on your baby.

Down's syndrome

Poor muscle tone contributes to the tendency of some children with Down's syndrome to be physically inactive. For this reason, their need for physical stimulation is vital. (The guideline for hypotonicity, above, should be taken into account when massaging or using the yoga exercises.)

Most children generally love music, singing and dancing, and children with Down's syndrome are no different. Sensory stimulation (such as music) and motor stimulation (such as dance) should be a part of their education from a very early age. Movement stimulates the brain and nervous system. Music is composed of highly structured series of sounds and contains most of the elements of language — pitch, rhythm and timbre. Listening to music, singing along to nursery rhymes and dancing can help a baby with Down's syndrome acquire their language skills. Therefore, it is as important to sing, and use massage and yoga, with a baby who has Down's as it is with a baby who doesn't.

However, you should seek advice from your child's GP before commencing massage and yoga if your baby is suffering from internal organ defects.

Congenital malformation

A baby with a congenital malformation may benefit from receiving massage and yoga from infancy and into childhood, as it may help them have a positive self-image, as well as helping parents to overcome their fears and to accept their child's body shape more readily.

Practising massage and yoga safely

If your baby has any health problems, it is important that you consult your baby's specialist or GP before commencing the massage routine and yoga exercises. Some children with special needs have the added challenge of medical illnesses to contend with as well. For example, many children with Down's syndrome have a heart or circulatory condition. Massage and yoga increase blood flow, which potentially increases the volume of blood flow through the heart, arteries and veins. Therefore, it is important that the specialist is consulted to confirm that massage and yoga can be introduced.

Introducing massage when your baby is very sensitive

Not all babies are able to respond positively to a full massage or yoga routine; particularly if they are inclined to be very sensitive and become upset easily. With all babies it is important to only do the amount of massage or yoga that they are happy with, but with more sensitive babies it may be necessary to give a little more consideration to how the routines may be adapted to suit their needs.

If you have noticed that your baby is generally quite sensitive, it is advisable to introduce them to massage before the yoga routine. In the main, massage gives more opportunity for a parent to keep their baby in close contact with them. The yoga routine is not only far more energetic and possibly far too stimulating; it does not keep a sensitive baby close to their parent when doing some of the exercises. Yoga can be introduced at a later stage, when the baby is happy with a full massage and will be ready for the more stimulating yoga exercises.

It is beneficial if a parent is able to recognize the characteristics of their sensitive baby, which will help them to decide the best way to adapt the massage routine for them. The characteristics of sensitive babies mainly fall into three categories, these are commonly known as fussy, disorganized or hypersensitive babies. Although it is possible to give an indication of the main characteristic of a fussy, disorganized and hypersensitive baby, it is important to remember that all babies are individuals and the best way to really understand what a baby is 'saying' is to try to understand what they are trying to communicate through their non-verbal cues.

The fussy baby

When a baby is inclined to be fussy, the parents often feel that they have a particularly 'difficult' or 'demanding' child. A fussy baby is in fact desperate to be heard. The fussiness is an indication of a baby who is crying out to be calmed. They want to be able to feel safe and secure and are desperately seeking the level of care that is required so that they feel as if their needs for survival are being met.

How to tell if your baby is fussy:

- They are only content when they are in contact with you and cry when you put them down.
- They are extra-sensitive to disturbing noises.
- They do not adapt well to changes in their routine.

Things to remember when introducing massage to a fussy baby:

- Always be sensitive to your baby's cues.
- Introduce positive touch carefully and gradually – starting with the containment holds.
- Try massaging over your baby's clothes, until they feel more secure about being undressed.
- Choose a time in the day when your baby tends to be less fussy.
- Maintain close contact by massaging them whilst being held or across your lap.

The disorganized baby

'Disorganized' babies have often had a difficult and stressful birth, so they need help to become calm and to find an inner peace. Gentle rocking and soothing sounds may help a baby to become calm; as can swaddling, which may help them feel secure (see Chapter 6).

How to tell if your baby is disorganized:

- They are unable to maintain eye contact.
- They move their arms and legs in a fast, uncontrolled manner.
- They have distressed crying.
- They hold their hands in front of their face.
- They are prone to having hiccups.

Things to remember when introducing massage to a disorganized baby:

- It is best to introduce the massage routine whilst your baby is still dressed.

- Start slowly using the containment holds and as massage is introduced, keep your baby close to you.
- You can gradually increase the amount of strokes that you do with your baby.
- Lie your baby on their side during massage, which may reduce the over-stimulation of face-to-face contact.

The hypersensitive baby

Premature babies, babies with special needs and those that have experienced medical intervention at birth, may be hypersensitive, and may struggle to cope with over-stimulation and are inclined to become tired quickly.

How to tell if your baby is hypersensitive:

- They do not enjoy being cuddled and often give the impression that they would prefer to be left alone. They may even become distressed when someone tries to offer comfort.
- They try to avoid eye contact and often look fretful.
- They are easily disturbed and frightened.
- They may cry hysterically, often during the evening.

Things to remember when introducing massage to a hypersensitive baby:

- Ensure that the environment is calm and quiet.
- Dim the lighting.
- When your baby is ready for massage, start with the Newborn Routine.
- When your baby is accustomed to the Newborn Routine, introduce the long, gentle strokes from the massage routine keeping them clothed – all other strokes are likely to be too stimulating at this stage.
- When your baby is able to cope with skin contact, only uncover the area that is going to be massaged, so that your baby continues to feel secure.
- If the massage is too much for your baby, go back to the containment holds to reassure them.
- Avoid too much stimulation at any one time, for example avoid prolonged eye contact when massaging your baby.
- Handle your baby slowly and carefully, avoiding quick or sudden movements.

Activity

A containment hold for hypersensitive babies

Some babies may not cope with even the gentlest stroking, so before introducing the massage, start with the containment hold, which is calming and contains their positive energy.

Either with your baby lying on their back on a change mat or on your lap:

- gently rest a hand close to or on top of your baby's head
- rest the other hand underneath their feet
- remain still and quiet in this position for two or three minutes.

Special situations

Multiple births

Trying to incorporate baby massage into an already hectic daily routine for parents of twins or multiple births can be rather challenging, however, the following approaches will help to find a different way to achieve this.

- It may be a good idea to involve both parents, a willing grandparent or older sibling, should the babies be ready for a massage at the same time.
- The babies will be completely different and will display different cues, have different self-calming techniques, will enjoy different strokes and have different needs.
- The babies may wish to be massaged at different parts of the day, for instance one may prefer to be massaged in the morning whilst another prefers a massage after a bath and before bedtime.

Adoption/fostering

Touch is a universal language understood by children all over the world. Whether you are adopting from China, Romania, Russia or locally, you can express your feelings to your adopted child through touch. As this book explains throughout, positive touch communicates love, respect, safety and acceptance; all essential for a healthy parent–child relationship and there is no exception for adoptive or foster parents.

Whether for a newborn baby or a slightly older child, baby massage and yoga can really play an important part in successful adoption and fostering. The age and individual case needs to be considered carefully but massage and yoga can help to form trusting relationships and offer adoptive parents or foster parents a way to make up for lost time through quality contact time that promotes closeness, security and love. As bonding involves all the senses, but primarily touch, baby massage can really help in the bonding process and help you and your adopted child to become accustomed to each other. And don't forget that it will help your baby to feel nurtured and loved at a most unsettling time.

Positive touch, especially skin-to-skin contact and containment holding, can help bring a new baby closer to its adoptive/foster parents, especially when the baby will be grieving for the familiar touch, sounds or smells of their birth mother. When fostering, a gentle loving massage after visits to the birth mother in the very early days after separation can help with anxiety for both the baby and the foster parents. Involving siblings in the massage and yoga can help the new arrival to become accustomed to all their new family members.

> 'As time went on Chloe became anxious when being taken away from me for visits to her birth mother, whilst this was a positive sign that she was becoming attached to us, it was a difficult time for both of us as I did not like her having to experience such trauma as these visits had to happen. She would return to us quite irritable and massage helped to soothe her and me and we felt connected again.'

A stay in hospital

Parents whose children are admitted to hospital for investigations or surgery often feel isolated, scared and helpless, and as though they are losing control.

A gentle massage gives you the opportunity to give loving touch to your child and these anxieties will start to disappear. Massage also gives you something that you can have control of such as their care and general well-being and helps you to feel that you are able to do something positive for your child. It is so important for parents to maintain communication with their child whilst they are in hospital, so talking, smiling and singing nursery rhymes should be encouraged and indeed all of these can be done whilst massaging.

Often on special care baby units, there are specialist infant massage teachers who will show parents how to do positive touch with their baby safely. If the child is too poorly to be touched, parents may be offered the choice of learning the moves on a doll so that when their child is well enough they can then start to massage them. This also helps parents feel like they are doing something valuable for their critically ill baby and focus on something positive.

> 'Whilst massaging my daughter I felt the happiest of all the time I spent in hospital because of the contact and the fact that it relaxed us both. Apart from the obvious benefits the massage provided some light relief for both my daughter and myself, in what has been a traumatic experience.'
>
> Supplied by Debbie Mills, Hospital Play Specialist

Childhood ailments

Colds and snuffles

A blocked nose or 'snuffle' is common in babies under six months old. It is usually due to normal mucus that collects in the nose which is difficult for the baby to clear. Massage can help alleviate some of the symptoms. The measures listed below may help to ease the problem.

- Use the chest massage strokes and upper back strokes to help loosen mucus.
- Use the face massage strokes to help loosen and drain mucus from the sinuses. If you baby is old enough to sit up and support its own head then try the face massage with them sitting up to avoid the mucus blocking their airways.
- The Toe Rolling stroke works on the reflexology areas that correspond to the head, sinuses and teeth, so it may help to ease the congestion.

Colic, wind and constipation

Stomach discomfort from colic and wind can be very distressing for a baby, not to mention the parents. Chapter 2 explains the possible causes and symptoms of colic. Tummy massage and relaxation holds can be very beneficial for a baby suffering from colic and wind.

For relief of wind and colic follow the simple Colic Routine in Chapter 10 and the Lazy Lion Hold in Chapter 6. We recommend carrying out these strokes for a number of weeks as it will continue to alleviate this ongoing ailment.

> 'Laura was a bit constipated because she had just started solids and the tummy massage really helped with that. If anyone had told me beforehand that you can feel the congestion and help it on its way, I wouldn't have believed them – but it really worked, within a short while of the massage she had filled her nappy.'

Cradle cap

Cradle cap is flaky, dry skin that looks like dandruff, or thick, oily, yellowish or brown scaling or crusting patches. Although at its worst it may not look very pleasant, it is actually quite harmless. Most often it appears in the first few months of life, and it usually clears up on its own in about six to twelve months – although some children have it for several years.

For stubborn cases this remedy may help:

- Using the Angel Kisses stroke (see Chapter 13), rub a small amount of pure, natural oil, such as olive oil, on your baby's scalp and leave it on for about 15 minutes. (The oil helps to loosen dry flakes.) Take care when using olive oil as it can stain clothing.
- Gently comb out the flakes with a fine-toothed comb or brush them out with a soft brush.
- Wash your baby's scalp with a gentle baby shampoo afterwards and leave the shampoo on for a minute longer before rinsing, to help neutralize the oil. Washing ensures that the oil does not clog the pores and cause the flakes to stick, which might exacerbate the situation.

> 'Lucy developed only mild cradle cap, but still I thought it looked unsightly so I wanted to find a natural remedy to get rid of it. A health visitor recommended using olive oil, so before her sleep I massaged a small amount of olive oil into her hair and scalp. I placed an old towel in her cot to avoid the oil staining her sheet. When she awoke I was amazed at how easily the crusty flakes lifted from her head with her baby brush. I washed her hair thoroughly and it was gone. I did this once more a few weeks later and it never came back.'

Eczema and psoriasis

Dry skin is a common complaint and is one of the key symptoms in relation to conditions such as eczema and psoriasis. If your baby or child is suffering from mild eczema or psoriasis they may benefit from regular massage with a natural vegetable oil, which will help to moisturise their skin. It will help soothe and relax your baby, which in turn may improve their condition.

In severe cases, where the skin is broken, sore and inflamed, parents should refrain from massaging the infected skin. However, unaffected areas can be massaged as it keeps the rest of the skin moisturised and will help to calm an agitated baby.

Skin consultants recommend that emollient creams that are supplied to ease the itching and dryness of eczema should be applied in a light downward sweeping movement, following the direction of the hair growth, rather like applying butter to toast. This is so that the cream does not clog the follicles and so minimizes the risk of inflammation of the hair follicles. Therefore, it is **not** advisable to use the emollient cream for baby massage. The routines described in this book advise that the strokes go upwards towards the heart, working with the blood flow and the valves in the veins. In the main, this is against the direction of hair growth. To err on the side of caution it is suggested that parents follow guidelines for the application of the emollient and refrain from using it with baby massage to eliminate any risk of infection.

Sleep problems

Establishing a bedtime routine is extremely important for babies because they begin to know what to expect and start to feel secure and relaxed. Baby massage can be so beneficial in establishing this going-to-bed routine, for instance:

- bath
- massage with soothing music
- feed
- bedtime.

Refer to the section on Restful Sleep in Chapter 2 for further advice.

'I've gone back to work part-time and on those days when I can't be with her I make a point of giving her a massage before she has her bath at night. It's my way of saying that I've missed her.'

Teething

Teething and the appearance of their first little tooth is one of the great milestones of your baby's development. However, whilst your baby may sail through teething, there is a possibility that they might find it a most painful experience, causing distress to both you and your baby.

The following remedies may offer comfort on the arrival of those first new teeth:

- Extra hugs and cuddles will help comfort and reassure your baby if they are distressed.
- Gentle containment holding and stroking not only helps your baby to feel secure but can stimulate hormones to help your baby deal with the pain.
- The Toe Rolling Stroke (Chapter 09) and indeed the Finger Rolling Stroke (Chapter 11) work on the reflexology areas that correspond to the head, sinuses and teeth, so gentle massage of the hands and feet may help to ease the pain of teething.
- Try the Nose and Cheek Stroke (see Chapter 13) and follow the gum line, though take care to read your baby's cues as this area may be too painful to touch.
- If the area is not too swollen, lightly massage your baby's gum with a clean finger as, for some, this can be very soothing.

'We were going on holiday – a long car journey and James was teething; he was crying constantly and in terrible pain and I was worried that he would be in distress and I couldn't help him during the trip. At my baby massage class the teacher mentioned to us that toe rolling was really useful for colds and teething so I mentioned to her that we were going on a long journey in the car and I wanted to reduce James' discomfort. She suggested that I leave his shoes and socks off during the journey and lean my arm into the back of the car and roll his toes, especially when he was clearly in pain. It worked! The trip wasn't half as stressful as we'd thought and the massage really helped with James' pain.'

20

adapting massage for the growing child

In this chapter you will learn:
- how to keep growing babies and children interested in massage
- how to prepare for massage with an older child.

Adapting massage for the growing child

The gentle introductory stroking and massage routines in this book are aimed to be carried out from birth until your child reaches crawling age. However, this chapter offers advice and practical exercises on how to adapt the massage for a rapidly growing baby right through to adolescence.

Since massage has been introduced and enjoyed by both you and your baby it would indeed be a great shame to stop just because your growing baby is more interested in discovering all the new things around them, and are too busy to lie still long enough to have a full massage. However, by using different strategies you can continue this wonderful experience, especially as it is particularly important that positive touch is maintained during a child's life to help them feel loved, respected and increase their self-esteem.

Asking permission

When 'asking permission' is introduced to a baby, they learn very quickly that they can say 'no' and that they will be heard and their wishes respected. Asking permission to touch a child should never cease as the child is growing older. That way they learn that they can say 'no' to any type of touch they do not want to receive. They will be empowered to say what happens to them on a personal and physical level, which is a very important and valuable life skill for a child to learn. This may seem a little hard to imagine when you are looking at your 4 month old baby lying on their changing mat eager for a massage!

Key stages for adapting massage

Below are five key stages during your child's development that will require some adaptation to the massage sequence. Some points may be subtle, but they will all definitely enhance the massage experience for your growing child.

1 Babies around 6 months
2 The crawling stage
3 Toddlers
4 Pre-school children and beyond
5 Teenagers.

1. Babies around 6 months

As your baby is growing they naturally become more and more fascinated with their environment and what is going on around them. This is quite natural and you shouldn't feel despondent when your baby no longer gazes at you lovingly and interestingly. Indeed, this is rather an exciting time for both your baby and you and massage is still very important, so the original massage and exercise routines can be adapted somewhat to keep your baby's interest.

You can adapt the routine for this stage, as follows:

- Introduce some up-tempo rhymes into the massage and yoga exercises.
- Give them something to hold and look at whilst massage is taking place, such as a brightly coloured rattle or finger puppet.
- When massaging their back, put your baby across your lap (taking care to support their back – see correct positioning in Chapter 12) and lay a mirror on the floor so they can see their own reflection. Babies love to look at themselves and this will keep them amused whilst their back is being massaged.
- Try the leg, feet and/or tummy massage after each nappy change.
- Stroke their face or practise using the Angel Kisses stroke on their head during feeding, if it does not irritate or distract your baby.

2. The crawling stage

Don't feel disheartened when your baby does not appear interested in massage as they reach the crawling stage. It is simply because the world around them is just far too interesting and they are becoming rather more independent. Expect that in the middle of the massage their attention may shift to something new and exciting and they may turn over and crawl away!

You can adapt the routine for this stage, as follows:

- If your baby is still happy to be massaged whilst on the move, massage the areas that you can see or gain access to, such as their back, legs, feet or head.
- Make the massage more stimulating and maintain your baby's interest by introducing completely new nursery rhymes and music.

- Don't worry if you find massage time lasts only a few minutes, at about 18 months old babies usually become more agreeable to receiving a longer massage again.
- Use the yoga exercises which are more energetic, to keep your baby interested in positive touch and fun time play with you.

- Always remember to respect your baby's wishes.
- Initially they may have said 'yes' to massage but may soon change their mood minutes into the massage.
- Never force them to lie still when they would rather be off exploring.
- Reading your baby's non-verbal cues is still very important, but by now they are likely to be far more vocal, making it clear whether they want a massage or not.

---

3. Toddlers

Toddlers are growing in confidence, very much more independent, and not all will want to receive a full massage. Their attention span is much shorter than an older child's and they can become easily frustrated and tense if they have to stay still for any length of time. Toddlers will fiercely exert their independence, even turning to tantrums as their self-awareness increases; and by now they can verbally communicate whether they wish to receive a massage or not.

Adapting the massage and introducing the yoga exercises will introduce your toddler to new sensations and stimulate their very active imaginations. The key to keeping youngsters interested in massage and yoga is to make it fun and as enjoyable as possible. Parents should be reminded that they still ought to be very mindful of their child's non-verbal and verbal cues.

The following tips can enhance the massage and yoga routines for your toddler:

- Introduce their favourite nursery rhymes and songs into the massage and yoga routines; this may encourage them to sing along as well, making the activity all the more interesting for them.
- Name the parts of their body you are massaging, which helps with body awareness.

- Introduce props such as finger puppets and chiffon scarves to enhance sensations.
- Adapt the massage routine and the yoga exercises to only include the strokes and exercises they prefer, which will really boost their self-esteem.
- The inquisitive toddler may want to copy their parent and massage their favourite teddy or dolly after receiving massage themselves. This is great fun and encourages them to start to have an understanding of the concept of thinking about others, such as 'giving' and 'receiving'.

> Babies may remain interested in the yoga for some time beyond crawling as the exercises, by their nature, are more dynamic.

4. Pre-school children and beyond

The attention span of a three- or four-year-old child is much longer and they can now enjoy interactive games with parents, siblings and other children. Massage can really help stretch their imagination when you introduce some fun massage games. Your child may prefer not to remove their clothes completely; however massage games can still be beneficial, not least because it maintains the closeness massage time gives you both.

The following tips can enhance the massage for the pre-school child and children up to about ten years of age:

- Ask your child to choose where they want to be massaged, i.e. on their bed or a favourite, cosy spot in the house.
- Ask your child which massage strokes they would prefer each time, therefore empowering them and boosting their self-esteem.
- Use massage strokes to ease aching muscles and 'growing pains'.
- Children may wish to keep clothes on as they get older; massaging over their clothes is still beneficial.
- Story-telling whilst massaging can be great fun. Parents can use the stories included in Chapter 21, such as 'Making a Pizza' and 'Car Wash'. Try asking your child to use their imagination and come up with new stories, such as 'weather stories', 'planting a garden' or 'grooming a horse'. Use your child's hobby to inspire a massage game too – the list is

endless and can really help with their imagination and enhance their speech.

- Introduce props to help with cognitive development, for instance prepare a basket of food prior to performing the pizza massage. Smelling and touching slices of pepper, onion, mushroom, ham, etc. can enhance the physical massage game and turn it into a fun, learning experience.
- Children at this age often want to 'give' as much as they 'receive'. So encourage your child to massage you, their siblings or friends when they want to – this enhances their relationships and friendships; and respect for others.

The yoga routine will become more difficult as your child grows, so look out for Rhythm Kids™ exercise classes or children's yoga classes (or books), which will give you the opportunity to continue exercising with your child as they grow.

5. Teenagers

If your teenager has received regular massage since birth, they will have developed a special relationship with you and may still be amenable to receiving, and indeed giving a massage. However, this is a time when many children are body-conscious and may prefer to cover up when having a massage or they will only be prepared for certain areas of their body to be massaged that they are comfortable with exposing, such as feet, hands, head, neck and shoulders. Again, respect is the key to an enjoyable experience for both teenager and parent.

The massage, of course, will no longer be called baby massage and the strokes will need to be changed somewhat to accommodate larger limbs. Parents can rename the routine to suit the child, for example, a strapping son who plays football or rugby, may be more receptive to massage if it were called 'the post match rub down' or girls may prefer something like 'hockey match warm up'. Adapt what you call massage to fit with their individual needs, so as not to cramp their style!

As teenagers are dealing with surges in hormones and changes in body shape, many may become less communicative as they are approaching and going through puberty. Massage is an excellent way of finding some space in a busy day to help them relax and feel more comfortable with themselves. Also, it is often the case, when children feel more relaxed during the massage they are more inclined to open up to their parents and off-load any worries and anxieties they have. As with babies, massage remains a wonderful communication tool for you to use well into your child's adolescence.

Benefits for the older child:

- A back massage can be very effective for reducing stress, helping with relaxation and shoulder tension, insomnia, general aches and pains, breathing difficulties, skin problems and poor circulation (when combined with hands and/or feet massage).
- Leg massage helps with poor circulation, 'growing pains', hyperactivity, minor sports and play injuries, muscle fatigue, general stress and tension.
- Arm massage is good for easing aches, pains, skin conditions, cramp and tension.

Preparation for the massage routine for the growing child

- Prepare the environment to suit their needs. The older child may prefer a scented oil in the room.
- Ask the child to select their favourite relaxing music (be prepared for this to be different to what one might expect; a teenager may prefer rock music to a relaxing tune or classical music).
- Prepare the oil. A much older child may like a particular aromatherapy oil to help them relax. Always patch test this first before use and only buy aromatherapy oils from a reputable source or a qualified Aromatherapist.

Massage strokes used in the routine for the growing child

Effleurage

Effleurage is a commonly used massage stroke. It is used in the baby massage routine and is also suitable for the routine for the growing child.

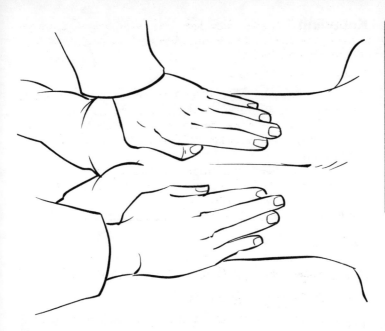

You can use the effleurage stroke to:

- introduce touch to your child
- put your child at ease
- warm and relax the muscle tissue prior to the deeper massage strokes
- increase the circulation
- stimulating peripheral nerves.

Effleurage is a soothing, gliding and long stroking movement using the palms of both hands on larger body areas or thumbs and fingers on small areas. It is an excellent stroke to indicate to your child which area is to be massaged and perfect for applying the massage oil.

This stroke is also used as a linking move between the different strokes and movements and should be light to begin with and firmer once your child is older.

Kneading

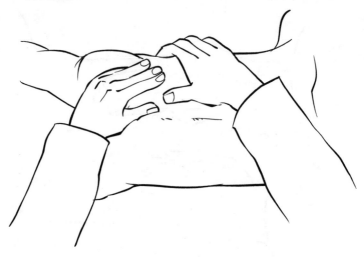

This massage movement is designed to work the more fleshy areas of the body and works more deeply than the effleurage stroke. The tissues in this area can be rolled and squeezed with the pads of the fingers and the thumbs. The pressure should be firm then relaxed and then repeated on another area.

You can use kneading to:

- release tension in your child's muscles
- help eliminate waste.

Frictions

Frictions are small circular movements made by the pads of the thumb or fingers. In adults this would be deep, but for a baby these frictions should be applied lightly.

You can use friction movement to:

- release tension in your child's muscles
- help eliminate waste.

CHILDREN

Your children are not your children.
They are the sons and daughters of life's longing for itself.
They come through you but not from you,
And though they are with you, yet they belong not to you.
You may give them your love, but not your thoughts,
For they have their own thoughts.
You may house their bodies but not their souls,
For their souls dwell in the house of tomorrow, which you
cannot visit, not even in your dreams.
You may strive to be like them, but seek not to make them
like you.
You are the bows from which your children as living arrows
are sent forth.
Let your bending in the archer's hand be for gladness.

Kahlil Gibran, *The Prophet*

21

story-time massage and massage routine for the growing child

In this chapter you will learn:
- how to make massage fun by introducing stories
- a massage routine for the growing child.

Using stories to make massage fun

Introducing stories when giving a child a back massage is great fun and can really stretch their imagination, help with speech and generally promote feelings of happiness and well-being. These stories can be done anywhere, providing the parent and child are comfortable, relaxed and that it is a good time for both.

Peer-to-peer massage is already being introduced into some UK schools and is where pupils, usually from the age of four and beyond, are encouraged to massage each other over clothes, on the back, neck, head and shoulders. This is supervised by a teacher and is accompanied with either soothing music or story-telling. Schools in Sweden have promoted this for many years now and studies carried out there show that pupils are more relaxed, can concentrate longer in class, are less aggressive towards one another and generally are more respectful of each other.

The story-time massages below can be used by parents, grandparents, siblings or friends.

Pizza massage

When a child asks for a 'pizza massage' they can be either lying down or straddled across a chair, facing backwards, with their head resting on their arms. Their partner stands or sits behind them.

It is important to ensure that one hand remains in touch with the child during the massage so they are not distracted if hands leave and then touch their body again, especially as they cannot see what is happening behind them.

- Begin by placing both hands on the shoulders of the child and ask them if they wish to be massaged today.
- The discussion about the ingredients for the pizza can begin
- Over the top of their clothes use sweeping effleurage movements with both hands up the back from the bottom, all over the back and down the sides of the back to simulate the rolling out of the pizza dough. Repeat three or four times.
- Now spread delicious tomato sauce over the dough, using effleurage strokes in a figure of eight, so it covers all of the back.
- Ask the child which toppings they would like on their pizza, for example:

- grated cheese
- mozzarella
- sliced onion
- olives
- ham slices
- pineapple
- sweetcorn
- pepperoni
- mushrooms
- slices of bell pepper
- spinach
- prawns
- anchovies
- chicken
- herbs
- drizzle of olive oil, etc.

- Each time they name an ingredient, become creative and simulate what it would be like to have that food on their back by making up a massage stroke. For example:
  - slices of pepper can be added to the pizza base by drawing small semi-circles all over the back with your index fingers
  - grated cheese can be simulated by drumming the finger tips very lightly all over the back
  - slices of pepperoni can be added by rubbing the back all over in small circular motions (frictions) with the pads of two fingers.
- Be as creative as possible with each of the ingredients that the child chooses for their pizza by using the effleurage, kneading and frictions movements.
- When the toppings are complete, rest cupped hands on their shoulders and use the kneading stroke lightly here.
- Effleurage the whole back again from the top to the bottom, to simulate opening the oven door.
- Slide the hands back to the shoulders to slide the pizza into the oven.
- Rest hands on shoulders for a moment whilst the pizza bakes in the oven.
- Then effleurage down the back again to open the oven door.
- Then effleurage up the back again to slide out the pizza.
- Thank the child for their contributions to the lovely pizza. Bon appétit!

Car wash massage

The car wash massage is another fun game to use when adapting the massage and gives your child the opportunity to move around a little, which is great for those that just can not sit still for very long! This game requires one or two 'car wash assistants', the child to be massaged is the 'car' that is in need of a little spruce up. The 'car wash assistants' can be parents, parent and sibling, siblings or friends. Ask your child to become their favourite car, ask them to describe what it looks like, what colour it is and what special features it has (this encourages your children to use their imagination and enhances language skills).

This is a guide for how to play the massage game, but it is by no means conclusive. You may adapt the game and make it as interesting and fun as possible!

- The 'car wash assistants' sit kneeling on the floor opposite one another with enough space between them for the little 'car' to drive in.
- Indicate to the 'car' that the car wash is now ready for them to drive in (on all fours in a crawling position).
- Encourage them to 'park' between the two assistants.
- Encourage your child to remain on all fours during the 'car wash' for maximum benefit.
- Both assistants rinse the whole of the 'car' from head to toe with long, sweeping effleurage movements, whilst explaining what is happening at each stage.
- Now cover the car with round sweeping movements, as though cleaning with soapy water and a large sponge.
- Pay particular attention to stubborn marks by using frictions, along the back (**do not put pressure on the spine**) and the fleshy parts of the limbs.
- Use kneading strokes on their arms and legs, taking care not to tickle.
- Use effleurage strokes to rinse the soap suds from the car and wipe away the water.
- Apply polish to the car and bring it to a shine making circular movements using the palms of the hands.
- Use Angel Kisses strokes on their head to clean the headlights.
- Finish with a last effleurage rub down to remove any last traces of polish.
- Ask the 'car' to drive out of the car wash ready for the next car.
- One of the assistants can now swap and become a 'car' of their choice for a gleaming new look!

One adaptation to try

Use the same principals for 'Grooming a Pony'. Simply let the car wash assistants become the grooms and the car is now the pony.

Happy grooming!

Massage routine for the growing child

Back massage

The positioning of your growing child for massage is much the same as it is for an adult. Place a large, soft towel on the bed/floor and ask your child to lie face down, head to one side, with arms either at their side or with hands tucked under their head. Cover the rest of their body with a towel for warmth and to protect modesty.

Kneel to one side of your child's body facing towards their head within comfortable reach of their back.

Some children prefer to receive a back massage whilst sitting cross-legged on the floor in front of their parent.

Applying the oil (if working 'skin-to-skin')

- Apply the oil to the palm of one of your hands.
- Warm oil between the hands.
- Work the oil over your child's back in large circular movements from the lower back to the shoulders.

Effleurage

- Using both hands, fingers pointing towards their head and facing inwards slightly, start from the top of the buttocks area.
- Gently and firmly stroke your hands up towards the shoulders, either side of the spine using as much of your hands as possible. **Avoid direct pressure on the spine.**
- At their shoulders, allow your hands to separate and draw down each side of the body, gently.
- Repeat six times.

Frictions

- Place both thumbs **either side of the base of their spine**, working the thumbs in a circular motion. Massage up to the shoulders, taking care not to rush. Sweep the hands over the shoulders and back down to the buttocks. Repeat three times.

- To add variety, effleurage a figure of eight on its side across the shoulder blades.

Effleurage

- Finish the back sequence with effleurage strokes from the buttocks to the shoulders.

Angel Kisses

- If your child is happy to have their hair tousled a little, the Angel Kisses stroke is a nice way to begin or end a back massage.

If preferred, follow the back routine from the Baby Massage Routine, omitting the extra strokes down the limbs.

Adapting strokes to suit rhymes and games makes the back massage a fun time for your child (see Pizza Massage).

The legs

The legs of an older child can be massaged with them lying on their backs, with a small pillow to support their head. Keep the rest of their body, which is not being massaged, covered with a soft blanket or towel for warmth. Place an old pillow under their knees, so as to relax the legs.

Applying the oil (if working 'skin-to-skin')

- Work the oil over the whole of one leg.

Effleurage

- Effleurage the whole leg from the ankle to the thigh using both hands.
- **Do not exert any pressure on the kneecap,** but gently sweep over the knee.

Kneading

- Knead the inside of the lower leg, as in baby massage, lifting the flesh to the centre of the shin, using your thumb.
- Massage from the ankle to the knee.
- Without using great pressure, knead the inside of the lower thigh.
- Knead the outer lower leg using your fingers working from the ankle to the knee.
- Knead the outside of the thigh.

Effleurage
- Finish the whole sequence by effleuraging the whole leg three times.
- On the final stroke incorporate the foot.

The foot

Effleurage
- Continue with the effleurage stroke on the foot three times.
- With the foot resting on your thigh, gently rotate the ankle three times both ways.
- Follow the strokes as explained in the Baby Massage Routine.

Now repeat the Leg and Foot massage on the other leg.

Abdomen massage

Follow the strokes as explained in the Baby Massage Routine. The knee hug could still be used on a toddler, but would become difficult to manage for an older child.

Chest massage

Follow the strokes as explained in the Baby Massage Routine. Be mindful that pubescent girls may no longer be happy with this part of the routine.

Arm massage

This massage can also be carried out whilst your child is sitting cross-legged on the floor facing you. This allows the opportunity for good communication.

Effleurage
- Gently holding your child's wrist, use the effleurage stroke to sweep gently up the inside of the arm from the wrist to the shoulder.
- Sweep down the outside of the arm to the wrist.
- Repeat six times.

Frictions
- Still supporting the arm, use the friction circular movements up the inner arm from the wrist to the crease of the elbow.
- Sweep your hand back to the wrist.
- Repeat this six times.

Kneading
- Gently knead the upper arm.

Effleurage
- Finish with effleurage strokes on the whole arm.

The hands
- Support their hand with the palm facing upwards.
- Apply deeper pressure using the principles of the Sole Stroke on the palm of the hand, paying particular attention to the ball of the thumb that can hold much tension in young students who've been writing in class all day.
- As with the Baby Massage Routine, thumb roll to the end of each finger, then rotate and gently pull.
- Finish the hand massage by sandwiching the hand between the palms of your hands.
- Hold this for a silent count of five.

Now repeat the Arm and Hand massage on the other arm.

The head and face
If your child is happy to have their hair touched, the Baby Massage Head and Face Routine is a lovely, relaxing way to end the massage.

Authors

Pauline Carpenter
Tel: 01889 566222
Email: pauline@touchlearn.co.uk
www.touchlearn.co.uk

Anita Epple
Tel: 01889 566222
Email: anita@touchlearn.co.uk
www.touchlearn.co.uk

Resources

Oils, music and books

All available from:

Touch Needs
Unit 2, Elms Farm Business Park
Bramshall
Staffordshire
ST14 5BE
Tel: 01889 560260
www.touchneeds.com

Baby massage oil

- Organic sunflower with vitamin E.
- Grape seed oil.
- Fractionated coconut oil.

Music

- *Music for Dreaming* – Designed specifically for relaxation and performed by the Melbourne Symphony Orchestra.

- *Playsongs* – Book and CD
- *Sleepy Time* – Play Songs

Books

- *Rhythm Kids* – Book and CD for music and movement with babies and toddlers, by Pauline Carpenter and Anita Epple.
- *The Little Book of Baby Massage*, by Pauline Carpenter and Lorraine Tolley.
- *Loving Hands* by Frederick Leboyer.
- *The Power of Touch*, by Phyllis K. Davis.
- *The Social Baby*, by Lynne Murray and Liz Andrews.
- *Baby Signs*, by Linda Acredolo & Goodwin.
- *Baby Minds*, by Linda Acredolo and Susan Goodwin.
- *Secrets of the Baby Whisperer*, by Tracy Hogg.
- *Mothering from the Heart*, by Bonnie Ohye.
- *Tao of Motherhood*, by Vimala McClure.

Helpful organizations

Touch-Learn Ltd

If you wish to find a *Rhythm Kids* or Infant Massage teacher in your area.

Tel: 01889 566222
Email: info@touchlearn.co.uk
www.touchlearn.co.uk

Guild of Infant and Child Massage

Supports professionals, parents, infants and children.

Tel: 01889 564555
www.gicm.org.uk

Association For Post-Natal Illness

Offers support to mothers suffering from post-natal illness.

Tel: 020 7386 0868
www.apni.org

Perinatal Illness UK

Offers support to mothers suffering from post-natal illness.

PO Box 49769
London, WC1H 9WH
Email: help@pni-uk.com
www.pni-uk.com

La Leche League

Offers support for breastfeeding mothers and their families.

Tel: 0845 456 1855
www.laleche.org.uk

National Childbirth Trust

Supports parents during pregnancy, birth and beyond.

Tel: 0870 444 8707
Breastfeeding Line: 0870 444 8708
Pregnancy and Birth Line: 0870 444 8709
www.nct.org.uk

Bliss

National charity for the welfare of the newborn baby.

Parent Support Helpline: 0500 618140
www.bliss.org.uk

The Active Birth Centre

Website with information on pregnancy, home and water birth,
breastfeeding, mother and baby care.

Tel: 020 7281 6760
www.activebirthcentre.com

Family Welfare Association

Helps families under stress achieve positive changes in their lives.

Tel: 020 7254 6251
www.fwa.org.uk

National Council for One-Parent Families

Promotes the welfare of one-parent families.

Tel: 0800 018 5026
www.oneparentfamilies.org.uk

Touch Research Institute

Institute devoted solely to the study of touch and its application in science and medicine.

University of Miami School of Medicine
PO Box 016820
Miami F1, 33101
Tel: 001 305 243 6790

The National Literacy Trust

Works in partnership with others to enhance literacy standards in the UK.
Tel: 020 7828 2435
www.literacytrust.org.uk

Parenting UK

A UK national body for professionals who work with parents.

www.parentinguk.org

BBC Parenting Newsletter

An online newsletter for parents.

www.bbc.co.uk/parenting/newsletter/

The Green Parent

Website supplementing the parenting magazine that is passionate about green issues and natural parenting.

www.thegreenparent.co.uk

Parentline Plus

A national charity that works for, and with parents by offering support during challenging times.

Tel: 0808 800 2222
www.parentlineplus.org.uk

Sure Start and Family Centres

A Government programme which aims to achieve better outcomes for children, parents and communities.

Tel: 0870 0002288
Email: info@dfes.gsi.gov.uk
www.surestart.gov.uk

Rhythm Kids

Anita and Pauline have also written Rhythm Kids, a beautifully illustrated book and CD of rhymes and fun-time exercises for you and your baby.

Why Sing Rhymes And Do Fun-Time Exercises With Your Baby?

The experiences in the first couple of years of life are so important for the overall development of an individual. During these formative years, parents can offer an enriching home environment for their child to learn in, by including singing and fun-time exercises as part of their daily routine.

Nursery rhymes are entrenched in history and form part of our linguistic traditions. When sung they can enhance synchronicity between parent and baby, as they are a wonderful communication tool allowing for enjoyable play time. In addition, research shows that they are also a powerful learning tool, because singing to children and encouraging them to join in, when they are able to, will actually be beneficial for the development of the brain.

The use of rhymes, when frequently repeated, plays a vital role in the development of language, even when the meaning of the words are not understood because a baby's memory is built through repeated experiences.

The beneficial element of singing rhymes is enhanced when accompanied by rhythmical exercises, which can help a child retain their flexibility, gain strength and improve muscle tone; as well as potentially improving co-ordination and balance. The art of balancing requires adequate muscle tone and postural control. The vestibular system (located in the inner ear) also plays an important role in our ability to balance. Movement is vital to the development of the vestibular system. So, it is important that babies are given the opportunity to move about and experience the world from different perspectives in order for the vestibular system to be stimulated.

When working through the fun-time exercises your baby will have the opportunity to experience play-time on the floor, in your arms and balanced on your legs. They will be able to see the world from all dimensions and feel what it is like to be turned around, swayed from side to side and lifted up and down. The rhymes and exercises allow you to help your baby learn, develop and play whilst having fun! Available from **www.touchneeds.com** and **www.amazon.co.uk**.